Rockin' the Classics and Classicizin' the Rock

Discographies
Series Editor: Michael Gray

Atlantic Records: A Discography
Compiled by Michel Ruppli

The Savoy Label: A Discography
Compiled by Michel Ruppli

The Prestige Label: A Discography
Compiled by Michel Ruppli

Brian Rust's Guide to Discography
Brian Rust

V-Discs: A History and Discography
Richard S. Sears

Melodiya: A Soviet Russian L.P. Discography
Compiled by John R. Bennett

The Chess Labels: A Discography
Compiled by Michel Ruppli

The Al Jolson Discography
Compiled by Larry F. Kiner

The Metropolitan Opera on Record: A Discography
of the Commercial Recordings
Compiled by Frederick P. Fellers

International Discography of Women Composers
Compiled by Aaron I. Cohen

Walter Legge: A Discography
Compiled by Alan Sanders

The Rudy Vallee Discography
Compiled by Larry F. Kiner

Rockin' the Classics and Classicizin' the Rock

A SELECTIVELY ANNOTATED DISCOGRAPHY

Janell R. Duxbury

Discographies, Number 14

GREENWOOD PRESS
Westport, Connecticut • London, England

Library of Congress Cataloging in Publication Data

Duxbury, Janell R.
  Rockin' the classics and classicizin' the rock.

  (Discographies, ISSN 0192-334X ; no. 14)
  Includes index.
  1. Rock music—Discographies. I. Title. II. Series.
ML156.4.R6D9 1985   016.7899'12454   84-22419
ISBN 0-313-24605-X (lib. bdg.)

Library of Congress Catalog Card Number: 84-22419
ISBN: 0-313-24605-X
ISSN: 0192-334X

First published in 1985

Greenwood Press
A division of Congressional Information Service, Inc.
88 Post Road West, Westport, Connecticut 06881

Printed in the United States of America

10 9 8 7 6 5 4 3 2 1

To music lovers everywhere

Contents

Preface

SCOPE

This selectively annotated discography documents the
intriguing connections between rock and classical music
genres. It is intended for browsing as well as for
researching reference questions. Rock music is an umbrella
term used somewhat loosely in this discography to define
music with a prominent beat and varying electronic instrumentation. The variants known as early rock and roll, pop
rock, progressive rock, reggae, synthesizer music, disco,
soul, and new wave are encompassed in this definition. The
term classical music refers to established works of the
major composers spanning the period from the Middle Ages
through the Twentieth Century and representing Europe, the
United States, and Latin America.
    After a general, historical introduction to the topic of
rock and classical connections, several major divisions
follow. Part I, "Rockin' the Classics," details numerous
examples of recorded rock instrumentals and songs from the
1950s to the present that borrow musical themes from the
classics. The classical essence varies widely from one
example to the next. At one extreme are contemporary
renditions of complete classical works that do not stray
noticeably from the original; at the other extreme are brief
classical quotes or phrases, subtly incorporated into rock
compositions, which require a very discerning ear. All
possible variations between these two extremes are represented in the entries. Part II, "Classicizin' the Rock,"
details recorded orchestral versions of songs originally
composed and/or recorded by rock musicians. Here the
musical style varies from strict classical interpretations
to pop-style orchestral renditions. Part III, "Other
Connections Between Rock and the Classics," includes a
compilation of recordings by rock groups or artists performing with established orchestras and choruses, live performances of rock groups or artists with orchestras before an
audience, selected examples of recorded rock music which
simulate a baroque or classical sound/structure, and examples of the manifest influence of rock on classical music.

Selected nonrock, historical background examples (e.g., Big Band, jazz, parody, and country/folk) are listed in several appendixes. A general index includes the names of classical composers, rock groups, rock artists, orchestras, choruses, orchestra conductors, sound recording producers, and song or instrumental titles.

Although Parts I and II are intended to be as comprehensive as possible, many other examples are still waiting to be discovered. Part III is selective rather than comprehensive and does not include all possible examples; it highlights those representative of the range of styles and performers which fall into these categories.

SOURCES

The best source of information about recorded music is the actual sound recording. When possible, I listened to and looked at records from my personal collection, radio station libraries, used record stores, and retail record stores. When the actual recording was unavailable, I consulted numerous music reference books.

Information on singles (45 rpm) was obtained from Paul C. Mawhinney's MusicMaster, the 45 RPM Record Directory: 1947 to 1982 (1983); Jerry Osborne's Popular & Rock Price Guide for 45's (1981); The Guinness Book of British Hit Singles (1981); Joel Whitburn's Billboard Book of Top 40 Hits, 1955 to Present (1983), Top Pop, 1955-1982 (1983), and Bubbling Under the Hot 100, 1959-1981 (1982).

Album details were gleaned from Terry Hounsome's New Rock Record (1983); Jerry Osborne's Record Albums (1982); Joel Whitburn's Top LP's, 1945-1972 (1973) and annual supplements; Schwann Record and Tape Guide (1971-); Gramophone Popular Catalogue (1976-); Directory of American Out-of-print LP Records (1983); Dictionary Catalog of the Rodgers and Hammerstein Archives of Recorded Sound (1981); Library of Congress Catalog: Music and Phonorecords (1953-72); National Union Catalog: Music, Books on Music, and Sound Recordings (1973-); Catalog of Copyright Entries: Sound Recordings (1972-); and Online Computer Library Center (OCLC) union catalog database.

Other information was discovered in reviews and articles in Rolling Stone, Melody Maker, Billboard, Variety, and others. Books of interest were Richard Meltzer's The Aesthetics of Rock (1970); Lillian Roxon's Rock Encyclopedia (1969); Dave Marsh's The Book of Rock Lists (1981); Barry Lazell's The Illustrated Book of Rock Records: A Book of Lists (1982); and Charles Reinhart's You Can't Do That!: Beatles Bootlegs & Novelty Records, 1963-80 (1981). In the case of obscure records, correspondence with record companies and record archives was an effective means of documenting album details.

ENTRY FORM

    In each of the three major parts of this discography the
names of groups and the surnames of individual artists are
listed alphabetically excluding initial articles. Under the
heading of each group or artist's name the numbered entries
are arranged alphabetically by song/instrumental or album
title and followed by relevant discographic details. In the
majority of main entries in Part I each song or instrumental
piece (whether from a single or album) is listed according
to its respective title. An album title is shown as the
main entry when its contents are based primarily on the same
classical source or when the titles of its individual
selections are repetitive, lengthy, or descriptive of the
source information. Main entries in Part II are listed by
album title and Part III reverts to mixed type entries.
Song or instrumental titles are enclosed in quotes (except
in content notes) and album titles are underlined.
    The order of discographic details follows the same
sequence in each entry: song/instrumental and/or album
title, year of release, recording company label name,
catalog number, and country where released. When a lower
case "c" appears before the year in an entry (e.g., c1973,
1974), it first designates the album copyright date and then
the year it was released. Single (45 rpm) releases issued
in conjunction with an album are listed after the album
details. Where possible both United States (US) and United
Kingdom (UK) release information is shown. US information
is generally listed first and UK, second. Release data for
other countries is given only when the recording was originally released outside the US or UK. The term "single"
refers to two-selection 45 rpm records; "album" refers to
multiselection 33 1/3 rpm LPs. The designation "EP" refers
to extended play records usually consisting of four to six
selections which may be either 45 rpm or 33 1/3 rpm.
    In Part I the composers and titles of the borrowed
classical themes are given as completely as possible.
Completeness and specificity of source information varies
since certain obscure recordings were not available.
Consequently it was occasionally impossible to identify and
verify the borrowed classical themes by listening to them.
In Part II where the sources of an album's selections are
mixed, the names of the rock groups or artists originally
performing the pieces are noted in parentheses. In Parts I
through III selective annotations add information such as
Billboard pop chart positions, Recording Industry Association of America (RIAA) million seller certifications for
singles, Grammy award nominations and winners, album contents, compilation and reissue data, and other facts of
interest.

LOOSE ENDS

There are usually unanswered questions in any comprehensive research project. Some of these loose ends are shared here with readers who may be able to provide additional information.

A number of albums or singles have been produced by performers with classically suggestive group names (e.g., Beethoven Soul, Offenbach, Ludwig and the Classics) which may or may not reflect classical underpinnings. Sample recordings were unavailable for these groups and for other song and instrumental titles that hint of classical connections. At this writing theme source information is unverified for the following examples of suggestive song and instrumental titles:

BUMBLE, B., AND THE STINGERS
    "Rockin'-on-'n'-off/Mashed #5." 1962 Rendezvous 174, US (single).
COOKE, SAM
    "Teenage Sonata." 1960 RCA 7701, US (single).
NEW YORK ROCK & ROLL ENSEMBLE
    "Orpheus." Reflections. 1970 Atco SD33-312, US.
REVERE, PAUL, AND THE RAIDERS
    "Paul Revere's Ride/Unfinished Fifth." 1961 Gardena 115, US (single).
    "1001 Arabian Nights." The spirit of '67. 1967 Columbia CS-9395, US.
ZAPPA, FRANK
    "Igor's Boogie." Burnt Weeny Sandwich. 1969 Reprise RS-6370, US.

Several concert reviews have mentioned various uses of classical themes but have failed to identify the specific connections to the existence of sound recordings. Some examples are:

DEEP PURPLE
    Saint-Saens' Bacchanale as an improvised guitar break, 1969
NICE
    Rachmaninoff's Concerto in C Sharp Minor, 1969 or '1970
    Lalo's Scherzo from Symphonie Espagnole, 1969 or 1970

Three rock versions of operas which were performed but not known to be recorded are:

Rock Mozart's Cosi fan Tutte, Hofstra University, 1970
Rock Carmen, London, 1972
Electronic Monteverdi's Poppea, New York Lyric Opera, Xenon Disco, 1982

Further details regarding the above listings as well as additions, corrections, or suggestions for this discography may be directed to Janell R. Duxbury, c/o Acquisitions Department, Memorial Library, University of Wisconsin, Madison, Wisconsin 53706.

Acknowledgments

Most of all I want to express my appreciation to my parents
Ruth and Don and my brother Jon for their patience and
untiring research assistance. I also want to thank several
other people and organizations for their excellent assis-
tance: my friend Janet for her encouragement; Ardella
Nelson (Quality Typing Service) for her cooperation and
expert wordprocessing skills; WORT-FM (especially John
Lindquist and John McDonald) and WIBA-FM (as Radio Free
Madison from 1969-1981) both in Madison, Wisconsin; WQFM-FM
in Milwaukee, Wisconsin; WXRT-FM in Chicago, Illinois;
University of Wisconsin-Madison Mills Music Library and
Memorial Library Interlibrary Loans; Bowling Green State
University Music Library; British Library National Sound
Archive; Madcity Music Exchange, Wazoo Records, Sugar Shack
Records, and Resale Records (all of Madison, Wisconsin);
Mike Cohen/Round and Round Records (of Milwaukee,
Wisconsin); Capitol Records; MCA Records, Inc.; Taft
Entertainment Company; and Phonogram Records (of Hilversum,
Netherlands). Finally of course, I thank all of the musical
artists and groups who produced, performed, and recorded the
music in this discography.

Introduction

At first hearing the average listener may be unaware of the
many links between rock music and the classics. One might
remember a few examples of "rockin' the classics" and pass
them off as interesting anomalies. However the pervasive
influence of the classics on rock music has grown from a
long line of precedents.

Each popular style of music in its day has produced
versions of the classics. Many composers throughout music
history have delighted in adding a "new" sound to familiar
melodies. The range and quality varies widely in these
attempts to blend the music of the past with the sounds of
the present and the future. Nonetheless the classical
"hook" draws in the listener with either distinct or vague
familiarity. Thus even the early days of ragtime and
vaudeville produced their own variations on the classics,
though we have few recordings. From the 1920s through the
1940s, James Price Johnson, Jelly Roll Morton, and Fats
Waller "jazzed up" the classics, alongside the Big Band
versions of Paul Whiteman, Duke Ellington, Harry James,
Tommy Dorsey, Glenn Miller, Les Brown, Gene Krupa, Woody
Herman, John Kirby, Freddie Martin, and Stan Kenton (see
Appendix A). James L. Limbacher's The Song List: A Guide
to Contemporary Music from Classical Sources (1973) highlights this era of classical borrowing.

During the 1950s and the 1960s the jazz genre produced
"jazzed up" classics by artists such as the Jacques Loussier
Trio, Dave Brubeck, and the Swingle Singers. Jazz interpretations continue to the present by artists such as Hubert
Laws and Herbie Mann (see Appendix B).

There have also been parodies of classical music
including those by Spike Jones, Peter Schickele, Anna
Russell, Portsmouth Sinfonia, and Allan Sherman (see
Appendix C). Even country and folk interpretations of the
classics have surfaced from time to time (see Appendix D).

Rock versions of the classics began in the early days of
rock and roll with the Elegants in 1958, Billy Storm in
1959, and Elvis Presley and Jackie Wilson in 1960. Others
followed by producing both rock versions of the classics and
the "Classical Rock" sound which imitated the classics
(e.g., New York Rock & Roll Ensemble; Left Banke). The

Beatles and the Rolling Stones led the way with simulated
baroque sounds. This trend continued to grow, culminating
in a frenzy of "Baroque Rock" during 1965-1969, peaking in
1967-1968. These years also marked the beginning of the
phenomenon of classical musicians performing baroque or
classical versions of rock music originally composed and/or
performed by rock musicians (e.g., Joshua Rifkin's The
Baroque Beatles Book). In fact baroque and rock meshed more
successfully than one might expect, since both genres share
contrapuntal structure and steady rhythmic patterns. The
"Classical Rock" or "Art Rock" style grew and matured into
the 1970s as it drew on classical style and technique while
relying on a rock beat and the use of electric instruments.
Through the magic of creative arrangements a mere handful of
rock musicians gave forth the lush sounds of a full-blown
orchestra. Rock groups which typified this style included:
Renaissance; Emerson, Lake & Palmer; Yes; Genesis; and
Electric Light Orchestra. This classical influence was also
reflected in the recordings of many other rock groups. The
"Rock Opera" phenomenon also emerged with the albums Tommy
and Jesus Christ Superstar. Beginning in the late 1960s the
development of synthesizers led to their use as substitutes
for strings. Ultimately whole orchestras were imitated in
the synthesized classics as played by Tomita. Although the
use of synthesizers continues to evolve, the inclusion of
string sections with rock bands is emerging again (e.g.,
China Crisis). This resurgence of an earlier trend shows a
continuing dimension in the influence of the classics on
rock music. The late 1970s and early 1980s have also
generated versions of the classics in the styles of disco
(e.g., Philarmonics), reggae (e.g., Jah Irie Chorus), and
new wave (e.g., Klaus Nomi; Lords of the New Church). These
developments have taken place in the United States, England,
and in continental Europe.
    Rock versions of the classics have been popular on the
Billboard pop singles chart throughout the history of rock
music. Walter Murphy's "A Fifth of Beethoven" reached
number one on the chart. Number two spots were held by the
Toys' "A Lover's Concerto" and Eric Carmen's "All by
Myself." Many similar recordings also did very well.
Although classical purists might cringe, clearly the record-
buying public appreciates these records. In assessing the
frequency of particular classical themes in popular music,
J.S. Bach appears to be the all-time favorite composer.
Certain classical themes have been recorded numerous times
in a rock style. A good example is Rimsky-Korsakov's
"Flight of the Bumblebee," recorded in at least eleven
different versions by as many artists.
    In a possible attempt to legitimize rock music in the
eyes of the nonrock world, rock groups have often performed
with established orchestras and choruses or appeared on the
same bill with them. These collaborations occur both on
sound recordings and in live performances. The most
publicly accessible example of this cultural meeting
occurred as an NBC network television special on March 14,
1970, entitled "The Switched-on Symphony." The program

included appearances by the Los Angeles Philharmonic
Orchestra, Jethro Tull, Santana, Nice, Bobby Sherman, Jerry
Goodman, Los Angeles Master Chorale, Ray Charles,
Christopher Parkening, João Carlos Martins, and Pinchas
Zukerman.   The Bee Gees toured with a hired orchestra as
early as 1968.   Emerson, Lake & Palmer tried the same
approach for a concert tour in 1977, but it proved to be too
expensive and they dropped the orchestra after only fifteen
performances.   Another strange twist has been the use of
tape-recorded or live orchestral introductions just prior to
a rock band's appearance on the concert stage.   Examples of
these efforts to meld classical and rock genres are: Mott
the Hoople (Holst/Jupiter from The Planets); Steve Harley
and Cockney Rebel (Ravel/Bolero); David Bowie 1972 tour
(Walter Carlos' version of Beethoven/Symphony No. 9); Yes
(Stravinsky/Firebird); Elvis Presley (R. Strauss/Also Sprach
Zarathustra); Rolling Stones (Copland/Fanfare for the Common
Man); Queen 1977 tour (Tchaikovsky/1812 Overture).   Rock
musicians have also been quick to point out their classical
training.   Michael Kamen, Dorian Rudnytsky, and Martin
Fulterman of New York Rock & Roll Ensemble attended the
Julliard School of Music; three members of Electric Light
Orchestra were once members of the London Symphony Orchestra; Rick Wakeman of Yes and Annie Lennox of Eurythmics
attended the Royal Academy of Music in London; Thijs van
Leer of Focus attended the Amsterdam Conservatoire; and Pat
Benatar and Annie Haslam were opera trained.   Various
members of Ars Nova, Mothers of Invention, and First Edition
also had classical training.
     There is evidence that the classical world has also taken
notice of the rock world.   Leonard Bernstein has been quoted
in praise of the New York Rock & Roll Ensemble, the Beatles,
and the Who's Tommy, the rock opera which earned the dis-
tinction of playing the Met and other opera houses.   Since
the Henry Wood Promenade concerts began in 1895, the first
rock group to ever appear at the London Proms was Soft
Machine at Royal Albert Hall on August 13, 1970.   Pink Floyd
was the first rock group to perform at the Montreux Classical Music Festival on September 18, 1971.   Emerson, Lake &
Palmer's Works, Volume 1 was reviewed in the classical,
rather than the rock, section of Stereo Review.   Both
established orchestras (e.g., the London Symphony Orchestra)
and pop-style orchestras (e.g., 101 Strings) have recorded
their own quasi-classical orchestral arrangements of rock
music originally composed and/or recorded by rock musicians.
Examples of "classicizin' the rock" show an array of
Beatles' compositions as the most popular choice for this
blend of the new with the old.   In a double twist the Royal
Philharmonic Orchestra recorded disco versions of the
classics in the Hooked on Classics series which was popular
and sold strongly.   Orchestras have used other rock trap-
pings for their "straight" versions of the classics (see
Part IIID).   Some symphony orchestras have added rock-style
laser and light shows to their concerts.   Performers such as
Virgil Fox and his "heavy organ" arrangements of Bach used
light shows in rock venues (e.g., Winterland at San

Francisco) as well as in "legitimate" venues (e.g., Carnegie
Hall).

The packaging of classical albums has, at times, imitated
that of rock albums (see Part IIID2). In the period between
1969 and 1973 both Columbia and RCA Red Seal released
"Greatest Hits" albums by most of the major classical
composers. Columbia's Greatest Hits of 1720, ...1721, and
...1790 featured album covers with Billboard-like pop charts
listing the contents. London Records' Orphic Egg composer
series chose unconventional album titles (e.g., Bach's Head,
Ravel's Head, etc.) for at least eight different classical
composers. Although the versions of these composers' music
were "straight," rock critics supplied hip street-talk liner
notes for some, and artists created psychedelic album
covers. In a parallel manner artists have reproduced works
of great art intact or in altered form on scattered rock
album covers. In contrast to Walter Carlos' Switched-on
Bach, Columbia also released Switched-off Bach, which
featured straight versions of the same pieces used on
Carlos' synthesizer album. Compilations of straight versions of classical pieces once used for rock interpretations
were released by Columbia (Joy! The Great Composers' Hits
for the '70s) and RCA Red Seal (Heavy Hits: Great Music That
Inspired Today's Hits and Joy: Great Classics That Inspired
Great Pop and Rock Hits of the '60's and '70's). In 1978,
the Philadelphia Orchestra employed rock star David Bowie as
a narrator on a recording of Peter and the Wolf (see Part
IIID3). The first rock-style picture-disc of classical
music appeared in 1979 in France as Front Populaire,
featuring various classical orchestras.

Present day classical composers have been slow to admit
the influence of rock music on their compositions. One
exception is Hans Werner Henze, who mentioned that he was
inspired by the Rolling Stones for his 1968 secular cantata
Musen Siziliens (see Part IIID1). Avant-garde experimental
composers such as Philip Glass and Glenn Branca have inte-
grated rock rhythm, repetition, and heavy amplification in
their works. Philip Glass released rock-style videos of
sections of his album The Photographer.

A final note involves some controversy over rock versions
of the classics. Added to the scorn of classical purists is
the furor over failure to give credit to the classical
composers. Some rock groups are very scrupulous about this
courtesy while others do not give credit at all. When
Emerson, Lake & Palmer failed to acknowledge Bela Bartok and
Leos Janacek on their first album, several magazine articles
denounced this omission. Their later albums usually ac-
knowledged their sources and they added Janacek to the
credits of their 1979 live album version of "Knife-Edge,"
which appeared originally on their first album. In England,
the controversy has been more prominent because the British
Broadcasting Corporation (BBC) has from time to time banned
tunes lifted from the classics. In fact Tomita's 1976 album
The Planets was actually banned for sale and use in the
United Kingdom after a 1977 court injunction was awarded to
Gustav Holst's daughter. She objected to the synthesizer

version of her father's composition.   This album is
available outside England.
    Whether used for reference and research or for browsing,
the following selectively annotated discography identifies
and documents further details of the fascinating profusion
of connections between rock and classical music genres.

Rockin' the Classics and Classicizin' the Rock

I.
Rockin' the Classics

ALL ELECTRIC ORCHESTRA

001 <u>Peter and the wolf</u>. 1977 TIL Records TIL-508.

Source: Prokofiev/Peter and the wolf, op. 67
Note: "Synthestrations" on this album are by David Merrill.

ANIMALS

002 "Bring it on home to me." <u>Animal tracks</u>. 1965 MGM SE-4305, US/ 1965 Columbia 33SX1708, UK (albums); 1965 MGM 13339, US/ 1965 Columbia DB-7539, UK (singles).

Source: Berlioz/La damnation de Faust, op. 24, part 3, Faust's aria (scene 8)
Note: The Animals' version of Sam Cooke's original song, loosely based on Berlioz, reached #32 on the Billboard pop singles chart. The song also appears on the compilations <u>The best of the Animals</u> (1966 MGM SE-4324) and <u>The best of the Animals</u> (1973 Abkco AB-4226). <u>See also</u> Sam Cooke

APHRODITE'S CHILD

003 "Rain and tears." <u>End of the world/Rain and tears</u>. 1968 Vertigo 6333-008 (album); 1968 Philips 40549, US/ 1968 Mercury MF-1039, UK (singles).

Source: Pachelbel/Canon in D major
Note: The very first release of a single was probably issued by Philips in France, where it reached #1 on their charts. In England, it reached #27 on the charts. However, in the United States, it passed virtually unnoticed. The song, arranged by group member Vangelis, also appears on the compilations <u>Best of Aphrodite's Child</u> (1975 Mercury 6333-002, Vertigo 6583-025) and <u>Greatest hits</u> (1981 Fontana 6420-006). A reissue of the original album, <u>Rain and tears</u>, was released (1975 Vertigo 6483-035).

APOLLO 100

004   "Air for the G string." <u>Joy</u>. 1972 Mega M31-1010,
        US.

        Source: J. S. Bach/Suite no. 3 in D major for
        orchestra, BWV 1068, Air for the G string
        Note: This piece appears as "Air on a G string" on
        the compilation <u>Classical gas</u> (198? Music for Pleas-
        ure MFP-50526, UK).

005   "Beethoven 9." <u>Master pieces</u>. 1972 Mega M51-5005,
        US.

        Source: Beethoven/Symphony no. 9 in D minor, op.
        125, mvt. 4, first theme
        Note: This instrumental also appears as the single
        "Song of joy" (1977 Eurogram 5002, US) and as "Joy
        (Beethoven 9)" on the compilation <u>Classical gas</u> (198?
        Music for Pleasure MFP-50526, UK).

        "Danse macabre." <u>See</u> "Evil midnight"

006   "Evil midnight." <u>Joy</u>. 1972 Mega M31-1010, US.

        Source: Saint-Saens/Danse macabre, op. 40
        Note: This piece appears as "Danse macabre" on the
        compilation <u>Classical gas</u> (198? Music for Pleasure
        MFP-50526, UK).

007   "Exercise in A minor." <u>Classical gas</u>. 198? Music
        for Pleasure MFP-50526, UK.

        Source: ?

        "In the hall of the mountain king." <u>See</u> "Mad moun-
        tain king"

        "Jesu, joy of man's desiring." <u>See</u> "Joy"

008   "Joy." <u>Joy</u>. 1972 Mega M31-1010, US (album); 1972
        Mega 0050, US (single).

        Source: J. S. Bach/Jesu, joy of man's desiring (from
        cantata no. 147).
        Note: This instrumental reached #6 on the Billboard
        pop singles chart and was nominated in 1972 for the
        pop instrumental Grammy award. It appears as "Jesu,
        joy of man's desiring" on the compilation <u>Classical
        gas</u> (198? Music for Pleasure MFP-50526, UK).

        "Joy (Beethoven 9)." <u>See</u> "Beethoven 9"

009   "Listening to Mozart." <u>Classical gas</u>. 198? Music
        for Pleasure MFP-50526, UK.

        Source: Mozart

010 "Mad mountain king." Joy. 1972 Mega M31-1010, US.

     Source: Grieg/Peer Gynt suite no. 1, op. 46, mvt. 4
     (In the hall of the mountain king)
     Note: This instrumental appears as "In the hall of
     the mountain king" on the compilation Classical gas
     (198? Music for Pleasure MFP-50526, UK).

011 "Mendelssohn's 4th." Joy. 1972 Mega M31-1010, US.

     Source: Mendelssohn/Symphony no. 4 in A, op. 90,
     mvt. 2
     Note: This instrumental reached #94 on the Billboard
     pop singles chart. It also appears on the compila-
     tion Classical gas (198? Music for Pleasure MFP-
     50526, UK).

     "Nutcracker." See "Nutrocker"

012 "Nutrocker." Master pieces. 1972 Mega M51-5005, US.

     Source: Tchaikovsky/Nutcracker suite, op. 71a, March
     of the wooden soldiers
     Note: This instrumental also appears as "Nutcracker"
     on the compilation Classical gas (198? Music for
     Pleasure MFP-50526, UK) and as "Nutrocker" on the
     compilation Telstar (198? Music for Pleasure MFP-
     5574, UK).

013 "Opus 5." Master pieces. 1972 Mega M51-5005, US.

     Source: ?

014 "Sonata 8." Classical gas. 198? Music for Pleasure
     MFP-50526, UK.

     Source: ?

     "Song of joy." See "Beethoven 9"

015 "Swan lake." Classical gas. 198? Music for Pleasure
     MFP-50526, UK.

     Source: Tchaikovsky/Swan lake, suite from the
     ballet, op. 20a

016 "Tristesse." Master pieces. 1972 Mega M51-5005, US.

     Source: Chopin/Etude in E, op. 10, no. 3
     Note: This instrumental also appears on the compila-
     tion Classical gas (198? Music for Pleasure MFP-
     50526, UK).

017 "William Tell." Master pieces. 1972 Mega M51-5005,
     US (album); 1977 Eurogram 5002, US (single).

Source: Rossini/William Tell overture
Note: This instrumental also appears on the compilation Classical gas (198? Music for Pleasure MFP-
50526, UK).

ARS NOVA

018 "Aquel caballero." Ars Nova. 1968 Elektra EKS-
74020, US.

Source: Anonymous Spanish Renaissance music

019 "Messe Notre Dame." Ars Nova. 1968 Elektra EKS-
74020, US.

Source: Guillaume, de Machaut/La messe de Nostre
Dame

020 "Vita de l'Almamia." Ars Nova. 1968 Elektra EKS-
74020, US.

Source: Monteverdi

021 "Zarathustra." Ars Nova. 1968 Elektra EKS-74020,
US.

Source: R. Strauss/Also sprach Zarathustra, op. 30

AUGER, BRIAN, AND THE TRINITY

022 "Adagio per archi e organo." Befour. 1970 RCA
Victor LSP-4372, US/ 1970 RCA SF-8101, UK.

Source: Albinoni/Adagio in G minor for strings and
organ

023 "Pavane." Befour. 1970 RCA Victor LSP-4372, US/
1970 RCA SF-8101, UK.

Source: Fauré/Pavane, op. 50

AXELROD, DAVID

024 Messiah. 1971 RCA Victor LSP-4636, US.

Source: Handel/Messiah
Note: These rock interpretations by chorus and
orchestra of nine thematic segments from Handel were
arranged by David Axelrod.

B. BUMBLE AND THE STINGERS. See BUMBLE, B., AND THE
STINGERS

BAROQUE POPS

025 Love Scarlatti. 1976 Columbia PC-33966, US.

Source: Scarlatti/Sonatas
Note: The contents of the album and the sonata
numbers on which they are based are: The king and
court (58), Feel the joy of spring (413), Morning
flight (422), Samba antigua (6), Night moods (475),
Sunday's best (188), Love Scarlatti (366), On a
lonely summer's day (187), Argento (381), Luminous
garden (263), The message (104). The rock and jazz
idioms use instruments such as drums, electric bass,
electric guitar, piano, strings, and woodwinds as
conducted by Ettore Stratta.

026   Viva Vivaldi!.   1974 RCA Red Seal ARL1-0442, US.

Source: Vivaldi/as listed below
Contents: Suite from the four seasons -- Flute
concerto in D, op. 10, no. 3 -- Concerto in E
(L'amoroso) -- Guitar concerto in D: Adagio --
Gloria: Allegro -- Mandolin Concerto in C: Adagio
-- Concerto grosso in D minor: Adagio -- Concerto in
G for 2 mandolins: Adagio.
Note: This album was reissued as The Vivaldi beat
(1982 RCA Gold Seal AGL1-4368, US).

BASS, SID

027   "Malagueña."   Moog España.   1969 RCA LSP-4195, US.

Source: Albeniz; Lecuona/Malagueña
Note: This is a moog synthesizer version of Spanish
classical music.

028   "Ritual fire dance."   Moog España.   1969 RCA LSP-
      4195, US.

Source: Falla/El amor brujo (ballet), Ritual fire
dance

BAXTER, LES

029   "Clair de lune."   Moog rock, greatest classical hits.
      1972 GNP Crescendo GNPS-2053, US.

Source: Debussy/Suite bergamasque, Clair de lune
Note: This and the following are moog synthesizer
versions of the classics.

030   "Fantasie impromptu."   Moog rock, greatest classical
      hits.   1972 GNP Crescendo GNPS-2053, US.

Source: Chopin/Fantasie impromptu, op. 66

031   "Grieg piano concerto."   Moog rock, greatest classi-
      cal hits.   1972 GNP Crescendo GNPS-2053, US.

Source: Grieg/Piano concerto in A minor, op. 16

032   "Nocturne." <u>Moog rock, greatest classical hits</u>.
      1972 GNP Crescendo GNPS-2053, US.

      Source: Borodin/Nocturne

033   "Polovetsian dance." <u>Moog rock, greatest classical
      hits</u>. 1972 GNP Crescendo GNPS-2053, US.

      Source: Borodin/Polovetsian dances from Prince Igor

034   "Prelude in C." <u>Moog rock, greatest classical hits</u>.
      1972 GNP Crescendo GNPS-2053, US.

      Source: J. S. Bach/Prelude in C

035   "Prelude in E." <u>Moog rock, greatest classical hits</u>.
      1972 GNP Crescendo GNPS-2053, US.

      Source: Chopin/Prelude in E

036   "Prelude in E minor." <u>Moog rock, greatest classical
      hits</u>. 1972 GNP Crescendo GNPS-2053, US.

      Source: Chopin/Prelude in E minor

037   "Rachmaninoff piano concerto no. 2." <u>Moog rock,
      greatest classical hits</u>. 1972 GNP Crescendo GNPS-
      2053, US.

      Source: Rachmaninoff/Piano concerto no. 2 in C
      minor, op. 18

BEACH BOYS

038   "Boogie woodie." <u>Surfer girl</u>. 1963 Capitol T-1981
      (mono), ST-1981 (stereo), US.

      Source: Rimsky-Korsakov/The legend of Tsar Saltan,
      first theme (Flight of the bumblebee)
      Note: This short instrumental was arranged by Brian
      Wilson. The album was reissued twice (1976 Capitol
      SM-1981; 1980 Capitol SN-16014, US). The piece was
      also included on <u>Instrumental Hits</u> (1965 Capitol
      CP-7396, Japan).

BEATLES

039   "All you need is love." <u>Magical mystery tour</u>. 1967
      Capitol MAL-2835 (mono), SMAL-2835 (stereo), US
      (albums); 1967 Capitol 5964, US/ 1967 Parlophone
      R-5620, UK (singles).

      Source: J. S. Bach/Two-part invention in F major
      (no. 8)
      Note: The first few measures of this Bach piece, as
      played on trumpet, appear as part of the montage at
      the end of the song. The single reached #1 on the
      Billboard pop singles chart and was an RIAA certified

million seller. The song also appears on 1967-1970
(1973 Apple [Capitol] SKBO-3404, US/ 1973 Parlophone
PCSP-718, UK) and Reel music (1982 Capitol SV-12199,
US/ 1982 Parlophone PCS-7218, UK).

040   "Because." Abbey Road. 1969 Capitol SO-383, US/
        1969 Apple PCS-7088, UK.

        Source: [rumored to be a backwards version of]
        Beethoven/Sonata no. 14 in C sharp minor, op. 27, no.
        2 (Moonlight sonata)
        Note: This rumor, alluded to by John Lennon himself,
        is untrue. However, the song does resemble that
        work's first movement in that it uses the same key
        signature, the Neapolitan or bII chord, an arpeg-
        giated structure, similar melodic rhythm and a shift
        to the major subdominant in the second phrase.

041   "I want to hold your hand." Meet the Beatles. 1964
        Capitol 2047, US (album); 1964 Capitol 5112, US/
        1963 Parlophone R-5084, UK (singles).

        Source: Gounod/St. Cecilia mass, credo section
        Note: The opening measures of the Beatles' song and
        the Gounod piece are similar, but no conscious
        connection was likely intended. The single reached
        #1 on the Billboard pop singles chart and was an RIAA
        certified million seller. The song also appears on
        1962-1966 (1973 Apple [Capitol] SKBO-3403, US/ 1973
        Parlophone PCSP-717, UK).

042   "In the Tyrol." Help!. 1965 Capitol SMAS-2386, US.

        Source: Wagner/Lohengrin, overture to act 2
        Note: In actuality, this sixth item on the Beatles'
        film soundtrack album was not played by the Beatles.
        It was arranged by Ken Thorne and played by the
        George Martin Orchestra.

BECK, JEFF

043   "Beck's bolero." Truth. 1968 Epic BN-26413, US/
        1968 Columbia SCX-6293, UK (albums); 1967 Epic
        10157 (B-side of "Hi ho silver lining"), 1968 Epic
        15-2278, US (singles).

        Source: Ravel/Bolero
        Note: This instrumental is loosely based on Ravel's
        style. Truth was later reissued as part of the
        double set Truth/Beck-ola (1977 Epic BG-33779, US).

BELLING, ANDY

044   New Messiah. 1972 Columbia KC-31713, US.
        Source: Handel/Messiah
        Note: Andy Belling arranged this new version of

Handel's "Messiah" and conducted the Revelation
Philharmonic Orchestra and the One Experience Choir.
The contents are: Overture -- Unto us a Child is
born -- Glory to God -- I know that my Redeemer
liveth -- And the glory of the Lord -- Hallelujah --
All we like sheep -- Surely He hath borne -- He
trusted in Him -- The trumpet shall sound -- Since by
man came death -- Hallelujah (reprise).

BENNINGHOFF'S BAD ROCK BLUES BAND

045 "B minor mass." Church Bach. 1972 SSS International
     17, US.

     Source: J. S. Bach/Mass in B minor

046 "Brandenburg concerto no 2." Church Bach. 1972 SSS
     International 17, US.

     Source: J. S. Bach/Brandenburg concerto no. 2 in F
     major, BWV 1047

047 "Cantata no. 80." Church Bach. 1972 SSS Inter-
     national 17, US.

     Source: J. S. Bach/Cantata no. 80

048 "Cantata no. 140." Church Bach. 1972 SSS Inter-
     national 17, US.

     Source: J. S. Bach/Cantata no. 140

049 "Do, Lord." Beethoven Bittersweet. 1971 SSS Inter-
     national 15, US.

     Source: Beethoven

050 "No. 3 error-attica." Beethoven Bittersweet. 1971
     SSS International 15, US.

     Source: Beethoven/Symphony no. 3 in E flat, op. 55
     (Eroica)

051 "No. 5 da-da-da-daah." Beethoven Bittersweet. 1971
     SSS International 15, US.

     Source: Beethoven/Symphony no. 5 in C minor, op. 67

052 "No. 6 boggy bayou revival." Beethoven Bittersweet.
     1971 SSS International 15, US.

     Source: Beethoven/Symphony no. 6 in F, op. 68
     (Pastoral)

053 "Prelude in C major." Church Bach. 1972 SSS Inter-
     national 17, US.

     Source: J. S. Bach/ Prelude in C major

054 "Prelude, rock, fugue in D minor." <u>Church Bach.</u>
     1972 SSS International 17, US.

     Source: J. S. Bach/Prelude and fugue in D minor

055 "Prelude, rock, fugue in F major." <u>Church Bach.</u>
     1972 SSS International 17, US.

     Source: J. S. Bach/Prelude and fugue in F major

056 "Saint Matthew passion." <u>Church Bach</u>. 1972 SSS
     International 17, US.

     Source: J. S. Bach/St. Matthew passion

BLACKMORE, RITCHIE. <u>See</u> RAINBOW

BLOOD, SWEAT & TEARS

057 "40,000 headmen." <u>3</u>. 1970 Columbia KC-30090, US/
     1970 CBS 64024, UK.

     Source: Bartok/Hungarian peasant songs, ballad;
     Prokofiev/Lieutenant Kije suite, op. 60
     Note: Two of the themes used in this arrangement are
     variations of the above classics.

058 "Variations on a theme by Erik Satie (1st and 2nd
     movements); Variation on a theme by Erik Satie (1st
     movement)." <u>Blood, Sweat & Tears</u>. 1969 Columbia
     PC(CS)-9720, US/ 1969 CBS 63504, UK.

     Source: Satie/Gymnopédie no. 1 (sometimes known as
     no. 3)
     Note: This album by Blood, Sweat & Tears opened and
     closed with these instrumentals. The instrumental
     received a 1969 Grammy nomination for instrumental
     arrangement and won the 1969 Grammy for contemporary
     instrumental.

BLUE OYSTER CULT

059 "Joan Crawford." <u>Fire of unknown origin</u>. 1981
     Columbia FC-37389, US/ 1981 CBS 85137, UK.

     Source: Grieg/Peer Gynt suite no. 1, op. 46, mvt. 4
     (In the hall of the mountain king)
     Note: In the ending of this song, one can hear some
     of the Grieg piece.

BUMBLE, B., AND THE STINGERS

060 "Bumble boogie." 1961 Rendezvous 140, US (single).

     Source: Rimsky-Korsakov/The legend of Tsar Saltan,
     first theme (Flight of the bumblebee)

Note: This instrumental reached #21 on the Billboard pop singles chart. <u>See also</u> Jools Holland; Morells; Nylons

061   "Nut rocker." 1962 Rendezvous 166, US/ 1962 Top Rank JAR-611, UK (singles).

Source: Tchaikovsky/Nutcracker suite, op. 71a, March of the wooden soldiers
Note: This instrumental, arranged by Kim Fowley and played by William Bumble et al, reached #23 on the Billboard pop singles chart in the U.S. and reached #1 on the British charts. It was rereleased in 1972 in both countries (1972 Rendezvous 166, US/ 1972 Stateside SS-2203, UK). This instrumental was nominated in 1962 for a Grammy in the category of rhythm and blues recording. Both this piece and the previous entry may have also appeared on the British EP <u>Piano stylings of B. Bumble</u> (19?? Stateside SE-1001, UK). <u>See also</u> Apollo 100; Emerson, Lake & Palmer; Jack B. Nimble and the Quicks; Tak Tiks

BYRDS

062   "She don't care about time." 1965 Columbia 43424, US (single).

Source: J. S. Bach/Jesu, joy of man's desiring (from cantata no. 147)
Note: The Bach piece appears as a guitar break in the middle of the song. The song was originally the B-side of the hit single "Turn, Turn, Turn." It wasn't put on an album until it was included on <u>The original singles, 1965-1967, volume 1</u> (1980 Columbia FC-37335, US).

CALE, JOHN

063   "Brahms." <u>The academy in peril</u>. 1972 Reprise MS-2079, US/ 1972 Reprise K-44212, UK.

Source: Brahms?

064   "Risé, Sam and Rimsky-Korsakov." <u>Music for a new society</u>. 1982 Ze PB-6019, US/ 1982 Island ILPS-7019, UK.

Source: Rimsky-Korsakov/Piano concerto in C sharp minor, op. 30, mvt. 3
Note: An orchestra playing the piano concerto, filtered to sound like it's on the radio, is heard underneath a spoken vocal by Risé Cale.

CARLOS, WALTER (WENDY)

065   "Air on a G string." <u>Switched-on Bach [I]</u>. 1968 Columbia MS-7194, US.

Source: J. S. Bach/Suite no. 3 in D major for
orchestra, BWV 1068, Air for the G string
Note: This moog synthesizer album reached #10 on the
Billboard pop album chart and #1 on the classical
chart. The album won 1969 Grammy awards for classical album of the year, classical performance by
instrumental soloist without orchestra, and best
engineered classical recording. This particular
piece also appears on Best of Carlos (1983 CBS 74110,
UK).

066 "Brandenburg concerto no. 1 in F major." Switched-on
     Brandenburgs, vol. I. 1980 Columbia M2X-35895, US.

Source: J. S. Bach/Brandenburg concerto no. 1 in F
major, BWV 1046
Note: This album is the first to be released under
Walter Carlos' new name, Wendy Carlos. The album was
reissued as half-speed mastered (1982 CBS Masterworks
HM-45950, US).

067 "Brandenburg concerto no. 2 in F major: first
     movement." By request. 1975 Columbia M-32088, US.

Source: J. S. Bach/Brandenburg concerto no. 2 in F
major, BWV 1047
Note: The entire concerto appears on Switched-on
Brandenburgs, vol. II (1980 Columbia M2X-35895, US).
That album was reissued as half-speed mastered (1982
CBS Masterworks HM-45951, US).

068 "Brandenburg concerto no. 3 in G major." Switched-on
     Bach [I]. 1968 Columbia MS-7194, US.

Source: J. S. Bach/Brandenburg concerto no. 3 in G
major, BWV 1048
Note: This concerto's first movement was released as
a Walter Carlos single (1969 Columbia 4-44803, US)
and the final movement as a track on Bach's greatest
hits, vol. 1 (1969 Columbia MS-7501, US). The entire
concerto appears on Switched-on Brandenburgs, vol. I
(1980 Columbia M2X-35895, US) and on Best of Carlos
(1983 CBS 74110, UK).

069 "Brandenburg concerto no. 4 in G major." The well-
     tempered synthesizer. 1970 Columbia MS-7286, US.

Source: J. S. Bach/Brandenburg concerto no. 4 in G
major, BWV 1049
Note: This concerto is also included on Switched-on
Brandenburgs, vol. II (1980 Columbia M2X-35895, US).
The album The well-tempered synthesizer above re-
ceived 1970 Grammy award nominations in classical
performance by instrumental soloist without orchestra
and best engineered classical recording. It reached
#199 on the Billboard pop album chart.

070   "Brandenburg concerto no. 5 in D major." <u>Switched-on</u>
      <u>Bach II</u>.   1973 Columbia KM-32659 US.

      Source: J. S. Bach/Brandenburg concerto no. 5 in D
      major, BWV 1050
      Note: This concerto is also included on <u>Switched-on</u>
      <u>Brandenburgs, vol. II</u> (1980 Columbia M2X-35895, US).

071   "Brandenburg concerto no. 6 in B flat." <u>Switched-on</u>
      <u>Brandenburgs, Vol. II</u>.   1980 Columbia M2X-35895,
      US.

      Source: J. S. Bach/Brandenburg concerto no. 6 in B
      flat, BWV 1051
      Note: This album was reissued as half-speed mastered
      (1982 CBS Masterworks HM-45951, US).

072   "Chorale prelude, wachet auf." <u>Switched-on Bach [I]</u>.
      1968 Columbia MS-7194, US.

      Source: J. S. Bach/Wachet auf (from cantata 140)

073   "Domine ad adjuvandum from 1610 vespers." <u>The well-</u>
      <u>tempered synthesizer</u>.   1970 Columbia MS-7286, US.

      Source: Monteverdi/Domine ad adjuvandum (from 1610
      vespers)

074   "La gazza ladra." <u>Clockwork orange</u>.   1972 Columbia
      KC-31480, US.

      Source: Rossini/La gazza ladra (The thieving magpie)
      Note: This instrumental also appears on <u>Best of</u>
      <u>Carlos</u> (1983 CBS 74110, UK).

075   "Jesu, joy of man's desiring." <u>Switched-on Bach [I]</u>.
      1968 Columbia MS-7194, US.

      Source: J. S. Bach/Jesu, joy of man's desiring (from
      cantata no. 147)
      Note: This instrumental also appears on <u>Best of</u>
      <u>Carlos</u> (1983 CBS 74110, UK).

076   "Little fugue in G minor." <u>By request</u>.   1975
      Columbia M-32088, US.

      Source: J. S. Bach/Fugue in G minor, BWV 578

077   "March." <u>Clockwork orange</u>.   1972 Columbia KC-31480,
      US.

      Source: Beethoven/Symphony no. 9 in D minor, op.
      125, mvt. 4
      Note: This piece also appears on the soundtrack
      album from the Stanley Kubrick film <u>A clockwork</u>
      <u>orange</u> (1972 Warner Bros. BS-2573, US), which reached
      #146 on the Billboard pop album chart.

078 "Ninth symphony, 2d movement." Clockwork orange.
     1972 Columbia KC-31480, US.

     Source: Beethoven/Symphony no. 9 in D minor, op.
     125, mvt. 2
     Note: The title "Suicide scherzo" is used on the
     film soundtrack of A clockwork orange (1972 Warner
     Bros. BS-2573, US).

079 "Orfeo suite." The well-tempered synthesizer. 1970
     Columbia MS-7286, US.

     Source: Monteverdi/Orfeo suite

080 "Pompous circumstances." By request. 1975 Columbia
     M-32088, US.

     Source: Elgar/Pomp and circumstance

081 "Preludes and fugues no. 7 in E flat major and no. 2
     in C minor from book I of the well-tempered
     clavier." Switched-on Bach [I]. 1968 Columbia
     MS-7194, US.

     Source: J. S. Bach/Well-tempered clavier, book I,
     preludes and fugues no. 7 and no. 2

082 "Selections from suite no. 2 in B minor." Switched-
     on Bach II. 1973 Columbia KM-32659, US.

     Source: J. S. Bach/Suite no. 2 in B minor for
     orchestra, BWV 1067

083 "Sheep may safely graze from cantata no. 208."
     Switched-on Bach II. 1973 Columbia KM-32659, US.

     Source: J. S. Bach/Sheep may safely graze (from
     cantata no. 208)

084 "Sinfonia to cantata no. 29." Switched-on Bach [I].
     1968 Columbia MS-7194, US.

     Source: J. S. Bach/Sinfonia to cantata no. 29

085 "Sonatas in G (L. 209), D (L. 164), E (L. 430), D
     (L.465)." The well-tempered synthesizer. 1970
     Columbia MS-7286, US.

     Source: Scarlatti/Sonatas (as above)
     Note: The sonatas in E and D also appear on Best of
     Carlos (1983 CBS 74110, UK)

     "Suicide scherzo." See "Ninth symphony, 2d movement"

086 "Suite from Anna Magdalena notebook." Switched-on
     Bach II. 1973 Columbia KM-32659, US.

     Source: J. S. Bach/Notebook for Anna Magdalena Bach

087   "Theme (Beethoviana)." <u>Clockwork orange</u>. 1972
        Columbia KC-31480, US.

        Source: Beethoven
        Note: This piece also appears on the film soundtrack
        album <u>A clockwork orange</u> (1972 Warner Bros. BS-2573,
        US) and on <u>Best of Carlos</u> (1983 CBS 74110, UK).

088   "Title music." <u>Clockwork orange</u>. 1972 Columbia
        KC-31480, US.

        Source: Purcell/Music for the funeral of Queen Mary
        Note: This piece also appears on the film soundtrack
        album <u>A clockwork orange</u> (1972 Warner Bros. BS-2573,
        US) and on <u>Best of Carlos</u> (1983 CBS 74110, UK).

089   "Three dances from nutcracker suite: Russian dance,
        dance of the sugar-plum fairy, dance of the reed
        pipes." <u>By request</u>. 1975 Columbia M-32088,
        US.

        Source: Tchaikovsky/Nutcracker suite, op. 71a

090   "Two-part inventions in A minor and A major."
        <u>Switched-on Bach II</u>. 1973 Columbia KM-32659, US.

        Source: J. S. Bach/Two-part inventions in A minor
        and A major

091   "Two-part inventions in F major, B flat major, and D
        minor." <u>Switched-on Bach [I]</u>. 1968 Columbia
        MS-7194, US.

        Source: J. S. Bach/Two-part inventions in F major, B
        flat major, and D minor

092   "Water music (bourrée, air, allegro deciso)." <u>The
        well-tempered synthesizer</u>. 1970 Columbia MS-7286,
        US.

        Source: Handel/Water music
        Note: This piece also appears on <u>Best of Carlos</u>
        (1983 CBS 74110, UK).

093   "Wedding march." <u>By request</u>. 1975 Columbia M-32088,
        US.

        Source: Wagner/Lohengrin, act 3, Bridal chorus

094   "William Tell overture." <u>Clockwork orange</u>. 1972
        Columbia KC-31480, US.

        Source: Rossini/William Tell overture
        Note: This piece also appears on the film soundtrack
        album <u>A clockwork orange</u> (1972 Warner Bros. BS-2573,
        US).

CARMEN, ERIC

095 "All by myself." <u>Eric Carmen</u>. 1975 Arista AL-4057,
     US/ 1976 Arista ARTY-120, UK (albums); 1975 Arista
     0165, US/ 1976 Arista 42, UK (singles).

     Source: Rachmaninoff/Piano concerto no. 2 in C
     minor, op. 18, mvt. 2, first theme B
     Note: The single, released Dec. 13, 1975, reached #2
     on the Billboard pop singles chart in 1976 and became
     an RIAA certified million seller.

096 "My girl." <u>Eric Carmen</u>. 1975 Arista AL-4057, US/
     1976 Arista ARTY-120, UK.

     Source: Rachmaninoff/Piano concerto no. 2 in C
     minor, op. 18, mvt. 1, second theme

CARPENTER, JOHN

097 "Engulfed cathedral." <u>Escape from New York</u>. 1981
     Varèse Sarabande STV-81134, US/ 1981 That's Enter-
     tainment TER-1011, UK.

     Source: Debussy/Preludes, book 1, no. 10 (The
     engulfed cathedral)
     Note: Carpenter's synthesizer music appears on this
     <u>Escape from New York</u> film soundtrack album.

COOKE, SAM

098 "Bring it on home to me." <u>The best of Sam Cooke,
     vol. 1</u>. 1962 RCA Victor LPM-2625 (mono), LSP-2625
     (stereo), US (albums); 1962 RCA 8036, US (single).

     Source: Berlioz/La damnation de Faust, op. 24, part
     3, Faust's aria (scene 8)
     Note: Based loosely on Berlioz, this single reached
     #13 on the Billboard pop singles chart and was a 1962
     Grammy nominee for rhythm and blues recording. It
     also appears on <u>This is Sam Cooke</u> (1970 RCA Victor
     VPS-6027, US) and the reissue of <u>The best of Sam
     Cooke</u> (198? RCA AYL1-3863, US). The single was
     reissued (197? RCA Gold Standard 0705). Another
     major version of this song was recorded by the
     Animals in 1965 (see 002). Some minor remakes of
     this song were: Bill Haley and the Comets (<u>Rock and
     roll</u> 1973 GNP Crescendo GNPS-2077, US); Rod Stewart
     (<u>Smiler</u> 1974 Mercury SRM-1-1017, US and <u>Best of Rod
     Stewart, vol. 2</u> 1977 Mercury SRM-2-7509, US); Van
     Morrison (<u>It's too late to stop now</u> 1974 Warner Bros.
     2BS-2760, US); Dave Mason (<u>Dave Mason</u> 1974 Columbia
     PC-33096, US and <u>Certified live</u> 1976 Columbia PG-
     34174, US); John Lennon (<u>Rock 'n' roll</u> 1975 Apple
     SK-3419, US); Wilson Pickett (<u>I'm in love</u> 1968
     Atlantic SD-8175, US).

CORIGLIANO, JOHN

  099 The naked Carmen: electric rock opera. 1970 Mercury
       SRM-1-604, US.

       Source: Bizet/Carmen
       Note: This production includes moog synthesizer,
       various instrumental soloists, vocal soloists (David
       Hess, Melba Moore, William Walker, et al), and the
       Detroit Symphony Orchestra. John Corigliano and
       David A. Hess produced and arranged the music.

COUGARS

  100 "Saturday nite at the duck pond." 1963 Parlophone
       R-4989, UK (single).

       Source: Tchaikovsky/Swan lake, suite from the
       ballet, op. 20a
       Note: This instrumental single reached #33 on the
       British charts.

CURVED AIR

  101 "Ultra-Vivaldi." Phantasmagoria. 1972 Warner Bros.
       BS-2628, US/ 1972 Warner Bros. K-46158, UK.

       Source: Vivaldi?
       Note: This synthesizer instrumental may be imitation
       Vivaldi. It is credited to members of the band.

  102 "Vivaldi" and "Vivaldi with cannons." Air condition-
       ing. 1970 Warner Bros. WS-1903, US/ 1970 Warner
       Bros. K-56004, UK.

       Source: Vivaldi?
       Note: These pieces, featuring violin, are credited
       to members of the band and may be imitation Vivaldi,
       but they are very convincing in style. A picture
       disc was also released (1970 Warner Bros. WSX-3012,
       US). See also Sky

DANNA, MYCHAEL

  103 A synthesized interpretation of classic pieces. 19??
       Polyphony magazine

DEEP PURPLE

  104 "River deep, mountain high." The book of Taliesyn.
       1968 Tetragrammaton T-107, US/ 1969 Harvest SHVL-
       751, UK.

       Source: R. Strauss/Also sprach Zarathustra, op. 30
       Note: The theme is mixed into the extended album
       version of the song.

DEODATO (Eumir Deodato)

105   "Also sprach Zarathustra (2001)." Prelude. 1972 CTI
      CTI-6021, US (album); 1973 CTI 12, US/ 1973 Creed
      Taylor CTI-4000, UK (singles).

      Source: R. Strauss/Also sprach Zarathustra, op. 30
      Note: This brass and synthesizer single reached #2
      on the Billboard pop singles chart after its release
      in early 1973, while the British single reached #7 on
      their chart. The single won a 1973 Grammy for pop
      instrumental. The album was reissued as 2001 (CTI
      CTI-7081, US).

106   "Jesu, joy of man's desiring." Knights of fantasy.
      1979 Warner Bros. BSK-3321, US.

      Source: J. S. Bach/Jesu joy of man's desiring (from
      cantata no. 147)
      Note: This version is the first part of a disco
      medley titled "Bachmania."

107   "Pavane for a dead princess." Deodato 2. 1973 CTI
      CTI-6029, US.

      Source: Ravel/Pavane for a dead princess

108   "Prelude to afternoon of a faun." Prelude. 1972 CTI
      CTI-6021, US.

      Source: Debussy/Prelude to afternoon of a faun

109   "Rhapsody in blue." Deodato 2. 1973 CTI CTI-6029,
      US (album); 1973 CTI 16, US (single).

      Source: Gershwin/Rhapsody in blue
      Note: The single reached #41 on the Billboard pop
      singles chart.

DUKOV, BRUCE

110   "Bach a 'Sinding." Departures: a classical journey.
      1983 CBS BFM-37816, US/ 1983 CBS 73650, UK.

      Source: J. S. Bach/Unaccompanied cello suite no. 1;
      Sinding/Suite for violin and orchestra, mvt. 2
      Note: Dukov performs on violin, backed by synthesiz-
      ers, voices and orchestra.

111   "Could it be magic?" Departures: a classical
      journey. 1983 CBS BFM-37816, US/ 1983 CBS 73650,
      UK.

      Source: Chopin/Prelude in C minor, op. 28, no. 20

112 "For Kreisler's sake." <u>Departures: a classical journey</u>. 1983 CBS BFM-37816, US/ 1983 CBS 73650, UK.

Source: Kreisler/Praeludium and allegro

113 "Heart-throb romance." <u>Departures: a classical journey</u>. 1983 CBS BFM-37816, US/ 1983 CBS 73650, UK.

Source: Sarasate/Zigeunerweisen, op. 20

114 "Meowski." <u>Departures: a classical journey</u>. 1983 CBS BFM-37816, US/ 1983 CBS 73650, UK.

Source: Wieniawski/Violin concerto no. 2 in D minor, op. 22 (and other of his works)

115 "Sad song rondo." <u>Departures: a classical journey</u>. 1983 CBS BFM-37816, US/ 1983 CBS 73650, UK.

Source: Saint-Saens/Introduction and rondo capriccioso, op. 28

116 "A variegated Maria." <u>Departures: a classical journey</u>. 1983 CBS BFM-37816, US/ 1983 CBS 73650, UK.

Source: Schubert/Ave Maria; Bach-Gounod/Ave Maria

117 "Viva Vivaldi." <u>Departures: a classical journey</u>. 1983 CBS BFM-37816, US/ 1983 CBS 73650, UK.

Source: Vivaldi/The four seasons, op. 8, no. 4 (winter)

EARTH BAND. <u>See</u> MANN, MANFRED, 'S EARTH BAND

EDDY, DUANE

118 "Velvet nights." 1968 Reprise 0690, US (single).

Source: Mozart/Piano concerto no. 21 in C, K. 467 (Elvira Madigan)
Note: This instrumental is the B-side of "Niki Hokey."

EDMUNDS, DAVE. <u>See</u> LOVE SCULPTURE

EKSEPTION

119 "A la turka." <u>5</u>. 1973 Philips PHS-700-002, US/ 1972 Philips 6423-042, Netherlands.

Source: Mozart/Piano sonata no. 11 in A major, K. 300i (331), mvt. 3 (Rondo alla turca)

Note: This instrumental also appears on the various greatest hits compilations of the Dutch band Eksep-tion (Best of Ekseption 197? Philips 6423-053; Classics 1973 Philips 6410-044; Classics in pop 1975 Philips 6423-079; Greatest hits 197? Philips 6677-025, 1975 Philips 6410-079, 1982 Philips 6423-490; Wereld-successen 1982 Philips 6624-063; Motive 1972 Philips 6375-363).

120 "Adagio." Beggar Julia's time trip. 1969 Philips
     PHS-600-348, US/ 1969 Philips 6314-001, UK/ 1969
     Philips 861-821-LCY, Netherlands.

     Source: Albinoni/Adagio in G minor for strings and
     organ
     Note: This also appears on various greatest hits
     compilations (see 119).

121 "Air." Ekseption. 1969 Philips PHS-600-334, US/
     1969 Philips 873-003-UBY, Netherlands.

     Source: J. S. Bach/Suite no. 3 in D major for
     orchestra, BWV 1068, Air for the G string
     Note: This also appears on various greatest hits
     compilations (see 119).

122 "Ave Maria." 00.04. 1971 Philips 6423-019, Nether-
     lands.

     Source: montage of J. S. Bach/Fugue in D minor; J.
     S. Bach, Gounod/Ave Maria; J. S. Bach/Prelude no. 1
     in C major, BWV 553

123 "Ave Maria." Back to the classics. 1976 Philips
     6410-129, Netherlands; 1976 Polydor 2393-167.

     Source: Schubert/Ave Maria (op. 52, no. 6)

124 "El barbero." Ekseption. 1975 Philips 9299-329
     (6677-025); originally on 1974 Philips 6832-077.

     Source: Rossini/Barber of Seville overture

125 "Bourrée." Mindmirror. 1975 Philips 6413-081,
     Netherlands.

     Source: J. S. Bach/Lute suite no. 1 in E minor, BWV
     996, Bourrée

126 "Concerto." Beggar Julia's time trip. 1969 Philips
     PHS-600-348, US/ 1969 Philips 6314-001, UK/ 1969
     Philips 861-821-LCY, Netherlands.

     Source: Tchaikovsky/Piano concerto no. 1 in B flat
     minor, op. 23
     Note: This also appears on various greatest hits
     compilations (see 119).

127 "Concerto for clarinet in A major." <u>Back to the</u>
     <u>classics</u>. 1976 Philips 6410-129, Netherlands; 1976
     Polydor 2393-167.

     Source: Mozart/Concerto for clarinet in A major, K.
     622

128 "Concerto for violin in E minor." <u>Back to the</u>
     <u>classics</u>. 1976 Philips 6410-129, Netherlands; 1976
     Polydor 2393-167.

     Source: Mendelssohn/Concerto for violin in E minor,
     op. 64

129 "Dance macabre opus 40." <u>Ekseption</u>. 1969 Philips
     PHS-600-334, US/ 1969 Philips 873-003-UBY, Nether-
     lands.

     Source: Saint-Saens/Danse macabre, op. 40

130 "The death of Åse." <u>Bingo</u>. 1974 Philips 6413-501,
     Netherlands.

     Source: Grieg/Peer Gynt suite no. 1, op. 46, mvt. 2

131 "The 5th." <u>Ekseption</u>. 1969 Philips PHS-600-334, US/
     1969 Philips 873-003-UBY, Netherlands.

     Source: Beethoven/Symphony no. 5 in C minor, op.
     67, mvt. 1 (plus some short fragments of other
     Beethoven, e.g. Moonlight Sonata)
     Note: This piece by the Dutch band Ekseption seems
     to have been a popular single in Europe. It also
     appears on various greatest hits compilations (see
     119). It is titled "Finale (the 5th)" on <u>5</u> (1973
     Philips PHS-700-002, US/ 1972 Philips 6423-042,
     Netherlands).

132 "Flight of the bumble-bee." <u>Trinity</u>. 1973 Philips
     6423-056, Netherlands.

     Source: Rimsky-Korsakov/The legend of Tsar Saltan,
     first theme (Flight of the bumblebee)

133 "Have mercy on me." <u>Back to the classics</u>. 1976
     Philips 6410-129, Netherlands; 1976 Polydor 2393-
     167.

     Source: J. S. Bach/Erbarme dich, BWV 244

134 "In a Persian market." <u>Ekseption</u>. 1975 Philips
     9299-329 (6677-025); originally on 1974 Philips
     6832-077.

     Source: Ketelbey/In a Persian market

135   "Introduction." <u>5</u>. 1973 Philips PHS-700-002, US/
      1972 Philips 6423-042, Netherlands.

      Source: Beethoven

136   "Italian concerto." <u>Beggar Julia's time trip</u>. 1969
      Philips PHS-600-348, US/ 1969 Philips 6314-001, UK/
      1969 Philips 861-821-LCY, Netherlands.

      Source: J. S. Bach/Italian concerto in F, BWV 971
      Note: This also appears on various greatest hits
      compilations (see 119).

137   "Eine kleine nachtmusik." <u>Back to the classics</u>.
      1976 Philips 6410-129, Netherlands; 1976 Polydor
      2393-167.

      Source: Mozart/Serenade no. 13 in G major, K. 525
      (Eine kleine nachtmusik)

138   "The lamplighter." <u>3</u>. 1970 Philips 6413-007; 1971
      Philips 6423-005, Netherlands.

      Source: J. S. Bach/Prelude and fugue in A minor, BWV
      543
      Note: This also appears on various greatest hits
      compilations (see 119).

139   "The Moldau." <u>Back to the classics</u>. 1976 Philips
      6410-129, Netherlands; 1976 Polydor 2393-167.

      Source: Smetana/Ma vlast, vitava no. 2 (The Moldau)

140   "On Sunday they will kill the world." <u>3</u>. 1970
      Philips 6413-007; 1971 Philips 6423-005, Nether-
      lands.

      Source: Rachmaninoff/Prelude in C sharp minor, op.
      3, no. 2

141   "Partita nr. 2 in C minor." <u>00.04</u>. 1971 Philips
      6423-019, Netherlands.

      Source: J. S. Bach/Partita no. 2 in C minor

142   "Peace planet." <u>3</u>. 1970 Philips 6413-007; 1971
      Philips 6423-005, Netherlands.

      Source: J. S. Bach/Suite no. 2 in B minor, BWV 1067,
      Badinerie
      Note: This also appears on various greatest hits
      compilations (see 119).

143   "Rhapsody in blue." <u>Ekseption</u>. 1969 Philips PHS-
      600-334, US/ 1969 Philips 873-003-UBY, Netherlands.

Source: Gershwin/Rhapsody in blue
Note: This also appears on various greatest hits
compilations (see 119).

144 "Ritual fire dance." <u>Ekseption</u>. 1969 Philips
PHS-600-334, US/ 1969 Philips 873-003-UBY, Netherlands.

Source: Falla/El amor brujo (ballet), Ritual fire
dance

145 "Romance." <u>Trinity</u>. 1973 Philips 6423-056, Netherlands.

Source: Beethoven/Romance for violin and orchestra
no. 2 in F major, op. 50

146 "Rondo." <u>3</u>. 1970 Philips 6413-007; 1971 Philips
6423-005, Netherlands.

Source: Beethoven/Concerto no. 3 in C minor, op. 37
Note: This also appears on various greatest hits
compilations (see 119).

147 "Sabre dance." <u>Ekseption</u>. 1969 Philips PHS-600-334,
US/ 1969 Philips 873-003-UBY, Netherlands.

Source: Khatchaturian/Gayne ballet, Sabre dance
Note: This appears as "Sabre dance '74" on <u>Bingo</u>
(1974 Philips 6413-501, Netherlands) and as "Sabre
dance" on various greatest hits compilations (see
119).

148 "Siciliano in G." <u>5</u>. 1973 Philips PHS-700-002, US/
1972 Philips 6423-042, Netherlands.

Source: J. S. Bach/Sonata no. 2 in E flat major,
mvt. 2 (Siciliano)
Note: This also appears on various greatest hits
compilations (see 119).

149 "Sonata for flute nr. 5 in F major." <u>Back to the
classics</u>. 1976 Philips 6410-129, Netherlands; 1976
Polydor 2393-167.

Source: Handel/Sonata for flute no. 5 in F major,
op. 1, no. 11

150 "Sonata in F major." <u>Back to the classics</u>. 1976
Philips 6410-129, Netherlands; 1976 Polydor 2393-
167.

Source: Vivaldi/Sonata no. 2 in F major

151 "Space I." <u>Beggar Julia's time trip</u>. 1969 Philips
PHS-600-348, US/ 1969 Philips 6314-001, UK/ 1969
Philips 861-821-LCY, Netherlands.

Source: J. S. Bach

152 "Theme from Abdelazor." Back to the classics. 1976
     Philips 6410-129, Netherlands; 1976 Polydor 2393-
     167.

     Source: Purcell/Abdelazer

153 "Toccata." Trinity. 1973 Philips 6423-056, Nether-
     lands.

     Source: J. S. Bach/Toccata and fugue in D minor, BWV
     538

154 Vivace." 5. 1973 Philips PHS-700-002, US/1972
     Philips 6423-042, Netherlands.

     Source: J. S. Bach/Concerto for violin and orchestra
     in A minor, BWV 1041, mvt. 1

ELECTRIC LIGHT ORCHESTRA

155 "In the hall of the mountain king." On the third
     day. 1973 United Artists UA-LA188-F, US/ 1973
     Warner Bros. K-56021, UK.

     Source: Grieg/Peer Gynt suite no. 1, op. 46, mvt. 4
     (In the hall of the mountain king)
     Note: The album was reissued (1978 Jet PZ-35525, US/
     1978 Jet LP-202, UK). The song was recorded live on
     The night the light went on (1974 United Artists
     UA-LA318, US/ 1974 Warner Bros. K-56058, UK).

156 "Roll over Beethoven." Electric Light Orchestra II.
     1973 United Artists UA-LA040-F, US/ 1973 Harvest
     SHVL-806, UK (albums); 1973 United Artists 173, US/
     1973 Harvest HAR-5063, UK (singles).

     Source: Beethoven/Symphony no. 5 in C minor, op. 67,
     mvt. 1, first theme
     Note: Only the introduction, which precedes the
     remake of Chuck Berry's song, is based on Beethoven.
     The album and single were reissued (1978 Jet PZ-
     35533, US (album); 1974 United Artists 513, 1978 Jet
     5152, US (singles). The single reached #42 on the
     Billboard pop singles chart. The song also appears
     on the compilation Olé ELO (1976 United Artists
     UA-LA630-G, 1978 Jet JZ-35528, US/ 1976 Jet LP-19,
     UK) and live on The night the light went on (1974
     United Artists UA-LA318, US/ 1974 Warner Bros.
     K-56058, UK).

ELECTROPHON

157 "Allegro." Further thoughts on the classics. 1977
     Polydor 2482-335.

     Source: ?

158 "Anitra's dance from Peer Gynt." Further thoughts on
     the classics. 1977 Polydor 2482-335.

Source: Grieg/Peer Gynt suite no. 1, op. 46, mvt. 3,
first theme (Anitra's dance)

159   "Arrival of the Queen of Sheba." Further thoughts on
the classics. 1977 Polydor 2482-335.

Source: Handel/Solomon, act III

160   "Flight of the bumblebee." Further thoughts on the
classics. 1977 Polydor 2482-335.

Source: Rimsky-Korsakov/The legend of Tsar Saltan,
first theme (Flight of the bumblebee)

161   "Girl with the flaxen hair." Further thoughts on the
classics. 1977 Polydor 2482-335.

Source: Debussy/Preludes, book 1, no. 8

162   "Hall of the mountain king." Further thoughts on the
classics. 1977 Polydor 2482-335.

Source: Grieg/Peer Gynt suite no. 1, op. 46, mvt. 4
(In the hall of the mountain king)

163   "Moto perpetuo." Further thoughts on the classics.
1977 Polydor 2482-335.

Source: Paganini/Moto perpetuo, op. 11

164   "None but the weary heart." Further thoughts on the
classics. 1977 Polydor 2482-335.

Source: Tchaikovsky/None but the lonely heart, op.
6, no. 6

165   "Sabre dance from Gayaneh." Further thoughts on the
classics. 1977 Polydor 2482-335.

Source: Khatchaturian/Gayne ballet, Sabre dance

166   "Serenade." Further thoughts on the classics. 1977
Polydor 2482-335.

Source: ?

167   "Skater's waltz." Further thoughts on the classics.
1977 Polydor 2482-335.

Source: Waldteufel/Skater's waltzes, op. 183, no. 1

ELEGANTS

168   "Little star." 1958 Apt 25005, US/ 1958 HMV POP-520,
UK (singles).

Source: Mozart/Variations in C, K. 265 [Twinkle,
twinkle little star; which some say he wrote in 1761
at age 5]

Note: This single reached #1 on the Billboard pop
singles chart. It appears on the compilations <u>Oldies
but goodies, vol. 5</u> (1971 Original Sound OSR-LPS-
8855, US) and <u>At the hop</u> (1978 ABC AA-1111/2, US).

EMERSON, LAKE & PALMER

169 "Abaddon's bolero." <u>Trilogy</u>. 1972 Cotillion SD-
      9903, Atlantic SD-19123, US/ 1972 Island ILPS-9186,
      1973 Manticore K-43505, UK.

      Source: Ravel/Bolero
      Note: This piece uses the beat and style of Ravel,
      but the main tune is somewhat different.

170 "Bach two part invention in D minor." <u>Works,
      volume 1</u>. 1977 Atlantic SD2-7000, US/ 1977
      Manticore K-80009, UK.

      Source: J. S. Bach/Two-part invention in D minor,
      no. 4

171 "The barbarian." <u>Emerson, Lake & Palmer</u>. 1971
      Cotillion SD-9040, Atlantic SD-19120, US/ 1970
      Island ILPS-9132, 1973 Manticore K-43503, UK.

      Source: Bartok/Allegro barbaro

172 "Canario." <u>Love beach</u>. 1978 Atlantic SD-19211, US/
      1978 Atlantic K-50552, UK.

      Source: Rodrigo/Fantasia para un gentilhombre,
      Canario

173 "The enemy god/Dances with the black spirits."
      <u>Works, volume 1</u>. 1977 Atlantic SD2-7000, US/ 1977
      Manticore K-80009, UK.

      Source: Prokofiev/Scythian suite, op. 20, mvt. 2
      Note: This instrumental also appears in a live
      version on <u>Emerson, Lake & Palmer in concert</u> (1979
      Atlantic SD-19255, US/ 1979 Atlantic K-50757, UK).

174 "Fanfare for the common man." <u>Works, volume 1</u>. 1977
      Atlantic SD2-7000, US/ 1977 Manticore K-80009, UK
      (albums); 1977 Atlantic 3398, US/ 1977 Atlantic
      K-10946, UK (singles).

      Source: Copland/Fanfare for the common man
      Note: This instrumental also appears on <u>Best of
      Emerson, Lake & Palmer</u> (1980 Atlantic SD-19283, US/
      1980 Atlantic K-50652, UK).

175 "Hoedown." <u>Trilogy</u>. 1972 Cotillion SD-9903,
      Atlantic SD-19123, US/ 1972 Island ILPS-9186, 1973
      Manticore K-43505, UK.

Source: Copland/Rodeo, Hoedown
Note: A live version of "Hoedown" appears on <u>Welcome back my friends to the show that never ends</u> (1974 Manticore MC3-200, US/ 1974 Manticore K-63500, UK) and the studio version also appears on <u>Best of Emerson, Lake & Palmer</u> (1980 Atlantic SD-19283, US/ 1980 Atlantic K-50652, UK).

176 "Jerusalem." <u>Brain salad surgery</u>. 1973 Manticore MC-66669, Atlantic SD-19124, US/ 1973 Manticore K-53501, UK (albums); 1973 Manticore K-13503, UK (single).

Source: Parry/Jerusalem
Note: This piece also appears on <u>Best of Emerson, Lake & Palmer</u> (1980 Atlantic SD-19283, US/ 1980 Atlantic K-50652, UK) and as a live version on <u>Welcome back my friends to the show that never ends</u> (1974 Manticore MC3-200, US/ 1974 Manticore K-63500, UK).

177 "Knife-edge." <u>Emerson, Lake & Palmer</u>. 1971 Cotillion SD-9040, Atlantic SD-19120, US/ 1970 Island ILPS-9132, 1973 Manticore K-43503, UK (albums); 1971 Cotillion 44106, US (single).

Source: Janacek/Sinfonietta, mvt. 1
Note: The single is the B-side of the hit "Lucky man." A live version of "Knife-edge" appears on <u>Emerson, Lake & Palmer in concert</u> (1979 Atlantic SD-19255, US/ 1979 Atlantic K-50757, UK). On this live album, credit is finally given to Janacek, after criticism for this omission on the original album.

178 "Nutrocker." <u>Pictures at an exhibition</u>. 1972 Cotillion ELP-66666, Atlantic SD-19122, US/ 1971 Island HELP-1, 1973 Manticore K-33501, UK (albums); 1972 Cotillion 44151, US (single).

Source: Tchaikovsky/Nutcracker suite, op. 71a, March of the wooden soldiers
Note: This remake of the B. Bumble and the Stingers version (see 061) reached #70 on the Billboard pop singles chart in 1972. It was recharted in January 1973 to #51.

179 "The only way." <u>Tarkus</u>. 1971 Cotillion SD-9900, Atlantic SD-19121, US/ 1971 Island ILPS-9155, 1973 Manticore K-43504, UK.

Source: J. S. Bach/Toccata in F and Well-tempered clavier, book I, prelude no. 6
Note: Bach's themes are used in the introduction and bridge only.

180 "Piano improvisations: fugue." Welcome back my
     friends to the show that never ends. 1974 Manti-
     core MC3-200, US/ 1974 Manticore K-63500, UK.

     Source: Gulda/Fugue

181 "Pictures at an exhibition." Pictures at an exhibi-
     tion. 1972 Cotillion ELP-66666, Atlantic SD-19122,
     US/ 1971 Island HELP-1, 1973 Manticore K-33501, UK.

     Source: Moussorgsky; Ravel/Pictures at an exhibition
     Note: The Moussorgsky based sections of this piece
     are: Promenade, The gnome, The old castle, The hut
     of Baba Yaga, The great gates of Kiev. The album was
     recorded live at Newcastle City Hall on March 26,
     1971 and was captured on film along with performances
     of "The barbarian," "Knife-edge," and "Nutrocker."
     The film Pictures at an exhibition was released by
     Crown-International in Britain in 1972 and in the
     U.S. in 1975. In 1972, the album was nominated for a
     Grammy in the category of pop instrumental perfor-
     mance by an arranger, composer, orchestra and/or
     choral leader. The album reached #10 on the Bill-
     board pop album chart. A shorter live version of
     "Pictures at an exhibition" appears on Emerson, Lake
     & Palmer in concert (1979 Atlantic SD-19255, US/ 1979
     Atlantic K-50757, UK). "The great gates of Kiev" is
     the B-side of the "Nutrocker" single (1972 Cotillion
     44151, US).

182 "Toccata." Brain salad surgery. 1973 Manticore
     MC-66669, Atlantic SD-19124, US/ 1973 Manticore
     K-53501, UK.

     Source: Ginastera/Piano concerto no. 1, mvt. 4
     Note: A live version of this appears on Welcome back
     my friends to the show that never ends (1974 Manti-
     core MC3-200, US/ 1974 Manticore K-63500, UK).

     "Two part invention in D minor." See "Bach two part
     invention in D minor"

ENO, BRIAN

183 "Three variations on the canon in D major by Johann
     Pachelbel: fullness of wind, french catalogues,
     brutal ardour." Discreet music. 1975 Antilles
     7030, US/ 1975 Obscure OB-4, Editions EG EGS-303,
     UK.

     Source: Pachelbel/Canon in D major

ESPERANTO

184 "Danse macabre." Danse macabre. 1974 A&M SP-3624,
     US/ 1974 A&M AMLH-63624, UK.

     Source: Saint-Saens/Danse macabre, op. 40

ESSEX, DAVID

   185 "Dea sancta." Stardust (film soundtrack). 1975
        Arista AL-5000, US.

        Source: Gounod/Dea sancta

FIREBALLET

   186 "Night on bald mountain (suite)." Night on bald
        mountain. 1975 Passport PPSD-98010, US.

        Source: montage includes Moussorgsky/Night on bald
        mountain; Debussy/Preludes, book 1, no. 10 (The
        engulfed cathedral)

FERRANTE AND TEICHER

   187 "Chopsticks." Classical disco. 1980 Liberty/United
        LT-980, US.

        Source: Borodin; Rimsky-Korsakov/Paraphrases for
        four hands
        Note: This album offers disco versions of the
        classics by duo pianos and orchestra.

   188 "Grieg's piano concerto." Classical disco. 1980
        Liberty/United LT-980, US.

        Source: Grieg/Piano concerto in A minor, op. 16,
        mvt. 1

   189 "Malagueña." Classical disco. 1980 Liberty/United
        LT-980, US.

        Source: Albeniz; Lecuona/Malagueña

   190 "Prelude in C# minor." Classical disco. 1980
        Liberty/United LT-980, US.

        Source: Rachmaninoff/Prelude in C sharp minor, op.
        3, no. 2

   191 "Rachmaninoff piano concerto no. II." Classical
        disco. 1980 Liberty/United LT-980, US.

        Source: Rachmaninoff/Piano concerto no. 2 in C
        minor, op. 18

   192 "Ritual fire dance." Classical disco. 1980 Liberty/
        United LT-980, US.

        Source: Falla/El amor brujo (ballet), Ritual fire
        dance

   193 "Sabre dance." Classical disco. 1980 Liberty/United
        LT-980, US.

        Source: Khatchaturian/Gayne ballet, Sabre dance

194 "Tchaikovsky piano concerto no. I." Classical disco.
     1980 Liberty/United LT-980, US.

     Source: Tchaikovsky/Piano concerto no. 1 in B flat
     minor, op. 23

195 "Wedding march." Classical disco. 1980 Liberty/
     United LT-980, US.

     Source: Wagner/Lohengrin, act 3, Bridal chorus

FLEETWOOD MAC

196 "Eyes of the world." Mirage. 1982 Warner Bros.
     1-23607, US/ 1982 Warner Bros. K-56952, UK (al-
     bums); 1982 Warner Bros. 29966, US (single).

     Source: Pachelbel/Canon in D major
     Note: The Pachelbel tune is used in the introduction
     and near the ending in an instrumental/vocal chorus.
     The single is the B-side of "Hold me."

FOGELBERG, DAN

197 "Same old lang syne." The innocent age. 1981 Full
     Moon KE2-37393, US/ 1981 Epic EPC-88533, UK (al-
     bums); 1981 Full Moon 50961, US (single).

     Source: Tchaikovsky/1812 overture, op. 49, second
     theme
     Note: The first few measures of the song's melody
     follow the Tchaikovsky tune. The ending includes the
     traditional tune "Auld lang syne." The single
     reached #9 on the Billboard pop singles chart. It
     also appears on Dan Fogelberg's Greatest hits (1982
     Full Moon QE-38308, US).

FOUR SEASONS

198 "Opus 17 (Don't worry 'bout me)." Second vault of
     hits. 1967 Philips 600221, US (album); 1966
     Philips 40370, US/ 1966 Philips BF-1493, UK (sin-
     gles).

     Source: Mozart
     Note: This single reached #13 on the Billboard pop
     singles chart and was reissued under the number 44018
     in the U.S. It also appears on the compilation
     Frankie Valli and the Four Seasons (1977 K-tel
     NU-9350, US).

FOX, CHARLES

199 "Seasons." 1980 Handshake WS8-5307, US (single).

     Source: Pachelbel/Canon in D major
     Note: This single reached #75 on the Billboard pop
     singles chart in 1981. The B-side is a straight

classical version of "Pachelbel's canon in D major,"
made popular by the 1980 film <u>Ordinary people</u>.

GLEESON, PATRICK

200 <u>Beyond the sun: an electronic portrait of Gustav
     Holst's The planets</u>. 1976 Mercury SRI-80000, US.

     Source: Holst/The planets, op. 32 (Mars, Venus,
     Mercury, Jupiter, Saturn, Uranus, Neptune)

GONZALEZ

201 "Rockmaninoff." <u>Haven't stopped dancin'</u>. 1978
     Capitol SW-11855, US/ 1979 Sidewalk SWK-2001, UK.

     Source: Rachmaninoff/Piano concerto no. 2 in C
     minor, op. 18, mvt. 2
     Note: The album previously was titled <u>Shipwrecked</u>
     (1977 Capitol SW-11855, US).

HARRIS, DON "SUGARCANE"

202 "Funk and Wagner." <u>Sugarcane</u>. 1970 Epic E-33027
     (26524), US.

     Source: Wagner/Der ring des Nibelungen, Die Walküre,
     Ride of the Valkyries
     Note: This piece uses electric violin and orchestra.

HASLAM, ANNIE

203 "Going home." <u>Annie in wonderland</u>. 1977 Sire
     SR-6046, US/ 1977 Warner Bros. K-56453, UK.

     Source: Dvorak/Symphony no. 9 (old no. 5) in E minor
     (from the New World), op. 95, mvt. 2 (largo)
     Note: Annie Haslam usually sings with the rock group
     Renaissance, but released this solo album. "Going
     home" backs her voice with brass choir, vocal choir,
     flute, percussion, and harp. Louis Clark of the
     Royal Philharmonic Orchestra did the brass and choir
     arrangements and plays the flute. Haslam's rock
     musician husband, Roy Wood, also contributed to the
     album.

HENDERSON, LUTHER

204 "Henderson and Sullivan." <u>Turned-on Broadway</u>. 1982
     RCA Red Seal AFL1-4327, US.

     Source: Gilbert and Sullivan
     Note: This piece contains Gilbert and Sullivan
     operetta excerpts arranged to a disco beat.

HOLLAND, JOOLS

205 "Bumble boogie." <u>Jools Holland and his millionaires</u>.
     1982 I.R.S. SP-70602, US/ 1981 A&M AMLH-68534, UK
     (albums); 1982 I.R.S. 9906, US (single).

     Source: Rimsky-Korsakov/The legend of Tsar Saltan,
     first theme (Flight of the bumblebee)
     <u>See also</u> B. Bumble and the Stingers

HOLLYWOOD SOUNDS ROCK MOVIE ORCHESTRA

206 "Aida." <u>Your favorite classics go s-s-swinging</u>.
     198? BiBi Music BBM-95, UK.

     Source: Verdi/Aida

207 "Barber of Seville." <u>Your favorite classics go
     s-s-swinging</u>. 198? BiBi Music BBM-95, UK.

     Source: Rossini/Barber of Seville

208 "Carmen." <u>Your favorite classics go s-s-swinging</u>.
     198? BiBi Music BBM-95, UK.

     Source: Bizet/Carmen

209 "Flying dutchman." <u>Your favorite classics go
     s-s-swinging</u>. 198? BiBi Music BBM-95, UK.

     Source: Wagner/The flying dutchman

210 "Der freischutz." <u>Your favorite classics go
     s-s-swinging</u>. 198? BiBi Music BBM-95, UK.

     Source: Weber/Der freischütz

211 "Magic flute." <u>Your favorite classics go
     s-s-swinging</u>. 198? BiBi Music BBM-95, UK.

     Source: Mozart/The magic flute

212 "Martha." <u>Your favorite classics go s-s-swinging</u>.
     198? BiBi Music BBM-95, UK.

     Source: Flotow/Martha

213 "Merry wives of Windsor." <u>Your favorite classics go
     s-s-swinging</u>. 198? BiBi Music BBM-95, UK.

     Source: Nicolai/The merry wives of Windsor

214 "Nabucco." <u>Your favorite classics go s-s-swinging</u>.
     198? BiBi Music BBM-95, UK.

     Source: Verdi/Nabucco

215   "Ondine." <u>Your favorite classics go s-s-swinging</u>.
      198? BiBi Music BBM-95, UK.

      Source: Ravel/Ondine

216   "Orpheus." <u>Your favorite classics go s-s-swinging</u>.
      198? BiBi Music BBM-95, UK.

      Source: Offenbach/Orpheus in the underworld

217   "Rigoletto." <u>Your favorite classics go s-s-swinging</u>.
      198? BiBi Music BBM-95, UK.

      Source: Verdi/Rigoletto

218   "Tales of Hoffman." <u>Your favorite classics go
      s-s-swinging</u>. 198? BiBi Music BBM-95, UK.

      Source: Offenbach/Tales of Hoffman

219   "Tannhauser." <u>Your favorite classics go
      s-s-swinging</u>. 198? BiBi Music BBM-95, UK.

      Source: Wagner/Tannhauser

220   "La traviata." <u>Your favorite classics go
      s-s-swinging</u>. 198? BiBi Music BBM-95, UK.

      Source: Verdi/La traviata

221   "Tzar und Zimmerman." <u>Your favorite classics go
      s-s-swinging</u>. 198? BiBi Music BBM-95, UK.

      Source: Lortzing/Tzar und Zimmerman

HOWE, STEVE

222   "Concerto in D - 2nd mvt." <u>The Steve Howe album</u>.
      1979 Atlantic SD-19243, US/ 1979 Atlantic K-50621,
      UK.

      Source: Vivaldi/Concerto in D minor, mvt. 2
      Note: Steve Howe is a former member of the rock
      group Yes and a current member of Asia.

JACK B. NIMBLE AND THE QUICKS. <u>See</u> NIMBLE, JACK B., AND THE
QUICKS

JAH IRIE CHORUS

223   "Sensimillia." <u>Yard style Christmas</u>. 1982 JGM (Joe
      Gibbs Music) JGML-6070, US.

      Source: Handel/Messiah, Hallelujah chorus
      Note: This is a reggae version of Handel with new
      lyrics. The chorus features Dean Fraser.

JETHRO TULL

224   "Bourée." <u>Stand up</u>. 1969 Reprise RS-6360, US/ 1969
      Island ILPS-9103, UK.

Source: J. S. Bach/Lute suite no. 1 in E minor, BWV
996, Bourrée
Note: The album, <u>Stand up</u> was reissued (1973
Chrysalis CHR-1042, US and UK). This instrumental is
also featured on <u>Repeat: the best of Jethro Tull,
vol. II</u> (1977 Chrysalis CHK-1135, US/ 1977 Chrysalis
CHR-1135, UK) and on the live album <u>Bursting out</u>
(1978 Chrysalis CH2-1201, US/ 1978 Chrysalis CJT4,
UK).

JOEL, BILLY

225 "This night." <u>An innocent man</u>. 1983 Columbia
     QC-38837, US/ 1983 CBS 25554, UK.

     Source: Beethoven/Sonata no. 8 in C minor, op. 13
     (Pathétique), mvt. 2, first theme
     Note: Only the chorus uses the Beethoven theme.

KASENETZ-KATZ SINGING ORCHESTRAL CIRCUS

226 "Blue Danube waltz." <u>Kasenetz-Katz Singing
     Orchestral Circus</u>. 1968 Buddah BDS-5020, US
     (album); 1969 Super K SK-14657, US (single).

     Source: J. Strauss/Blue Danube waltz, op. 317, no. 1
     Note: This is a studio group of the Buddah record
     rock roster produced by Jerry Kasenetz and Jeff Katz.

227 "Symphony no. 9." <u>Kasenetz-Katz Singing Orchestral
     Circus</u>. 1968 Buddah BDS-5020, US (album); 1969
     Super K SK-14657, US (single).

     Source: Beethoven/Symphony no. 9 in D minor, op. 125

KAZDIN, ANDREW (with Thomas Z. Shepard)

228 "Bolero." <u>Everything you always wanted to hear on
     the moog (but were afraid to ask for)</u>. 197?
     Columbia M-30383, US.

     Source: Ravel/Bolero

229 "Carmen: prelude to act I, habanera, introduction to
     act I." <u>Everything you always wanted to hear on
     the moog (but were afraid to ask for)</u>. 197?
     Columbia M-30383, US.

     Source: Bizet/Carmen

230 "España." <u>Everything you always wanted to hear on
     the moog (but were afraid to ask for)</u>. 197?
     Columbia M-30383, US.

     Source: Chabrier/España

231   "Malagueña." <u>Everything you always wanted to hear on the moog (but were afraid to ask for)</u>. 197? Columbia M-30383, US.

   Source: Albeniz; Lecuona/Malagueña

KINGSLEY, GERSHON

232   "Rhapsody in blue." <u>Switched-on Gershwin</u>. 19?? Avco AV-11004-598, US.

   Source: Gershwin/Rhapsody in blue
   Note: Kingsley plays an electronic keyboard synthesizer.

KOKOMO

233   "Asia major." <u>Asia minor</u>. 1961 Felsted FL-7513, US.

   Source: Chopin

234   "Asia minor." <u>Asia minor</u>. 1961 Felsted FL-7513, US (album); 1960 Felsted 8612 (Future 1023), US/ 1961 London HLU-9305, UK (singles).

   Source: Grieg/Piano concerto in A minor, op. 16, mvt. 1
   Note: J. Wisner's instrumental reached #8 on the Billboard pop singles chart.

235   "Evening concerto." <u>Asia minor</u>. 1961 Felsted FL-7513, US.

   Source: Tchaikovsky/Piano concerto no. 1 in B flat minor, op. 23

236   "For lovers only." <u>Asia minor</u>. 1961 Felsted FL-7513, US.

   Source: Schubert

237   "Moonlight madness." <u>Asia minor</u>. 1961 Felsted FL-7513, US.

   Source: Beethoven/Sonata no. 14 in C sharp minor, op. 27, no. 2 (Moonlight sonata)

238   "Sweet memories." <u>Asia minor</u>. 1961 Felsted FL-7513, US.

   Source: Liszt

KRAFT, JACK (with Larry Alexander)

239   <u>1812 overture, op. 49 & Nutcracker suite</u>. 1977 London SPC-21168, US.

```
          Source:  Tchaikovsky/1812 overture, op. 49; Nut-
          cracker suite, op. 71a
```

KRAFTWERK

240 "Franz Schubert." <u>Trans-Europe express</u>. 1977
     Capitol SW-11603, US/ 1977 Capitol E-ST-11603, UK.

     Source: Schubert?
     Note: This may be only an imitation of Schubert, but
     it does convey his style.

LLOYD-WEBBER, ANDREW

241 <u>Variations</u>. 1978 MCA MCA-3042, US/ 1977 MCA MCF-
     2824, UK.

     Source: Paganini/Caprice in A minor, op. 1, no. 24
     Note: A single, "Theme and variations: variation
     16," was released (1978 MCA MCA-40866, US/ 1978 MCA
     MCA-345, UK). There are 23 variations on the album.

LORD, JON

242 "Bach onto this." <u>Before I forget</u>. 1982 Harvest
     SHSP-4123, UK.

     Source: Bach?

LORDS OF THE NEW CHURCH

243 "New church." <u>The Lords of the New Church</u>. 1982
     I.R.S. SP-70029, US.

     Source: Bach/Toccata and fugue in D minor, BWV 538
     Note: This new wave song's introduction is based on
     the Bach piece, if one listens very closely.

LOVE SCULPTURE

244 "Farandole from l'Arlesienne." <u>Forms and feelings</u>.
     1970 Parrot PAS-71035, US/ 1969 Parlophone PCS-
     7090, UK (albums); 1970 Parrot 342, US (single).

     Source: Bizet/L'Arlesienne suite no. 2, Farandole
     Note: The U.S. single by Dave Edmunds et al is the
     B-side of "In the land of the few." "Farandole" also
     appears on <u>The classic tracks 1968/1972</u> (1974 One-Up
     OU-2047, UK).

245 "Sabre dance." <u>Forms and feelings</u>. 1970 Parrot
     PAS-71035, US/ 1969 Parlophone PCS-7090, UK (al-
     bums); 1968 Parrot 335, US/ 1968 Parlophone R-5744,
     UK (singles).

Source: Khatchaturian/Gayne ballet, Sabre dance
Note: This instrumental also appears on <u>The classic
tracks 1968/1972</u> (1974 One-Up OU-2047, UK).

MACKAY, ANDY

246   "Ride of the Valkyries." <u>In search of Eddie Riff</u>.
1974 Island ILPS-9278, 1977 Polydor 2302-064, UK.

Source: Wagner/Der ring des Nibelungen, Die Walküre,
Ride of the Valkyries
Note: Andy Mackay is a member of the rock group Roxy
Music.

MANILOW, BARRY

247   "Could it be magic?" <u>Barry Manilow</u>. 1973 Bell 1129,
US (album); 1974 Bell 45-422, US (single).

Source: Chopin/Prelude in C minor, op. 28, no. 20
Note: The song's piano introduction is based on the
Chopin piece. The album and single were reissued
(<u>Barry Manilow I</u>. 1975 Arista AL-4007, US [album];
1975 Arista 0126, US/ 1978 Arista ARIST-229, UK
[singles]). The single reached #6 on the Billboard
pop singles chart. The song also appears on <u>Barry
Manilow live</u> (1977 Arista AL-8500, US), <u>Barry Manilow
greatest hits</u> (1978 Arista A2L-8601, US), <u>Manilow
magic</u> (1982 Arista NU-9740, US), and <u>Barry live in
Britain</u> (1982 Arista ARTV-4, UK).

MANN, MANFRED

248   <u>Peter and the wolf</u>. 1976 RSO RS-1-3001, US.

Source: Prokofiev/Peter and the wolf, op. 67
Note: This rock version of the classic features
Manfred Mann, Alvin Lee, and Stephane Grapelli. It
was narrated by Vivian Stanshall (of Bonzo Dog Band)
and produced by Jack Lancaster and Robin Lumley.
Prokofiev is credited with seven of twenty-one
segments on the record.

MANN, MANFRED, 'S EARTH BAND

249   "Joybringer." 1973 Polydor 14205, US/ 1973 Vertigo
6059-083, UK (singles).

Source: Holst/The planets, op. 32, mvt. 4, second
theme (Jupiter, the bringer of jollity)
Note: The single reached #9 on the British charts,
but went nowhere in the U.S. It was included on the
compilation <u>1971-1973</u> (1977 Vertigo 9199-107, UK).

250   "Starbird." <u>The roaring silence</u>. 1976 Warner Bros.
BS-2965, US/ 1976 Bronze ILPS-9357, UK (albums);
1976 Warner Bros. WBS-8252, US (single).

Source: Stravinsky/Firebird suite
Note: The single is an edited version entitled
"Starbird no. 2" and is the B-side of the hit
"Blinded by the light." The album was reissued (1977
Bronze BSK-3055, US/ 1977 Bronze BRON-357, UK).

MANZAREK, RAY

251 Carmina burana. 1983 A&M SP-4945, US/ 1983 A&M
     AMLX-64945, UK.

Source: Orff/Carmina burana
Note: This former member of the Doors played keyboards and arranged this rock version of Orff's
secular cantata. Instrumentation includes piano,
organ, synthesizer, drums, guitar, bass, sax, and
flute. The album was produced by Philip Glass and
Kurt Munkacsi. A rock video was released in conjunction with the album. The contents of the album are:
[Destiny: ruler of the world] -- The wheel of
fortune (O fortuna) -- The wounds of fate (Fortune
plango) -- [Springtime] -- The face of spring (Veris
leta facies) -- Sunrise (Omnia sol temperat) --
Welcome (Ecce gratum) -- The dance (Tanz) -- Sweetest
boy (Dulcissime) -- If the whole world was mine (Were
diu werlt) -- [In the tavern] -- Boiling rage
(Estuans interius) -- The roasted swan (Olim lacus)
-- In the tavern (In taberna) -- [The court of love]
-- Love flies everywhere (Amor volat) -- A young girl
(Stetit puella) -- Come, my beauty (Veni veni venias)
-- The lovers (Blanziflor et Helena) -- [Destiny:
ruler of the world] -- The wheel of fortune (O
fortuna).

MARTHA & THE VANDELLAS

252 "Nowhere to run." Dance party. 1965 Gordy GLPS-915,
     US/ 1965 Tamla STML-11013, UK (albums); 1965 Gordy
     7039, US/ 1965 Tamla Motown TMG-502, UK (singles).

Source: Rachmaninoff/Piano concerto no. 3 in D
minor, op. 30, mvt. 1
Note: This song's tune is very loosely similar to
that of Rachmaninoff. The single reached #8 on the
Billboard pop singles chart and was later reissued
(19?? Motown 452). The song also appears on Greatest
Hits (1966 Gordy GLPS-917, 1981 Motown STMS-5042,
1983 Motown M5-204V1, US/ 1966 Tamla STML-11040, 1981
Tamla STMS-5042, UK) and on Anthology (1974 Motown
M7-778, US/ 1974 Tamla STML-12060, UK). Other minor
versions of the song (written by the Holland-Dozier-
Holland team) were recorded by Paradise Express (12"
disco single, Fantasy 153, US), Wild Cherry (Wild
Cherry 1976 Epic PE-34195, US) and Grand Funk (What's
funk? 1983 Full Moon 1-23750, US).

MORELLS

253 "Bumble boogie." <u>Shake and push</u>. 1982 Borrowed
        Records BORO-3302, US.

      Source: Rimsky-Korsakov/The legend of Tsar Saltan,
      first theme (Flight of the bumblebee).
      <u>See also</u> B. Bumble and the Stingers

MOTHERS OF INVENTION. <u>See</u> ZAPPA, FRANK

MUNICH MACHINE

254 "A whiter shade of pale." <u>A whiter shade of pale</u>.
        1978 Casablanca NBLP-7090, US (album); 1978 Oasis/
        Hansa OASIS-5, UK (single).

      Source: J. S. Bach/Suite no. 3 in D major for
      orchestra, BWV 1068, Air for the G string/ Wachet
      auf, BWV 140, no. 1 (Sleepers, awake)
      Note: This is an instrumental disco version of
      Procol Harum's song (see 324).

MURPHEY, MICHAEL

255 "Wildfire." <u>Blue sky, night thunder</u>. 1975 Epic
        KE-33290, US/ 1975 Epic EPC-80741, UK.

      Source: Scriabin
      Note: The alleged Scriabin piece only occurs as a
      piano introduction on the album version. It is
      deleted on the single, so information on the single
      is omitted here.

MURPHY, WALTER

256 "Afternoon of a faun." <u>Walter Murphy's disco-
        symphony</u>. 1979 N.Y. International BKL1-3506, US.

      Source: Debussy/Prelude to afternoon of a faun

257 "Bolero." <u>Walter Murphy's discosymphony</u>. 1979 N.Y.
        International BKL1-3506, US.

      Source: Ravel/Bolero

258 "Dance your face off." <u>Phantom of the opera</u>. 1978
        Private Stock PS-7010, US.

      Source: Beethoven/Sonata no. 8 in C minor, op. 13
      (Pathétique), mvt. 2, first theme

259 "A fifth of Beethoven." <u>A fifth of Beethoven</u>. 1976
        Private Stock PS-2015, US (album); 1976 Private
        Stock 45073, US/ 1976 Private Stock PVT-59, UK
        (singles).

Source: Beethoven/Symphony no. 5 in C minor, op. 67,
mvt. 1, first theme
Note: The U.S. single reached #1 on the Billboard
pop singles chart and was an RIAA certified million
seller. It was nominated in 1976 for the Grammy
category of pop instrumental. This popular disco
instrumental also appeared on the film soundtrack
album of Saturday night fever (1977 RSO RS-2-4001,
US). Walter Murphy produced an instructional film-
strip/cassette entitled Disco beat of the classics
(1977 Keyboard Publications) that explored this
Beethoven piece, as well as Rimsky-Korsakov,
Gershwin, and Tchaikovsky.

260 "Flight '76." A fifth of Beethoven. 1976 Private
     Stock PS-2015, US (album); 1976 Private Stock
     45123, US (single).

     Source: Rimsky-Korsakov/The legend of Tsar Saltan,
     first theme (Flight of the bumblebee)
     Note: The single reached #44 on the Billboard pop
     singles chart.

261 "Introduction." Phantom of the opera. 1978 Private
     Stock PS-7010, US.

     Source: J. S. Bach/Toccata and fugue in D minor, BWV
     538

262 "Malagueña." Walter Murphy's discosymphony. 1979
     N.Y. International BKL1-3506, US.

     Source: Albeniz; Lecuona/Malagueña

263 "Mostly Mozart." Walter Murphy's discosymphony.
     1979 N.Y. International BKL1-3506, US.

     Source: Mozart

264 "The music will not end." Phantom of the opera.
     1978 Private Stock PS-7010, US (album); 1978
     Private Stock 45197, US (single).

     Source: Mozart/Sonata in C, K. 545, mvt. 1, first
     theme

265 "A night at the opera." Phantom of the opera. 1978
     Private Stock PS-7010, US.

     Source: Beethoven/Symphony no. 9 in D minor, op.
     125, mvt. 4, first theme

266 "Nightfall." A fifth of Beethoven. 1976 Private
     Stock PS-2015, US.

     Source: Chopin/Prelude no. 4 in E minor

267   "The phantom of your dreams." Phantom of the opera.
      1978 Private Stock PS-7010, US.

      Source: Bach/Toccata and fugue in D minor, BWV 538
      Note: The break section of this song is based on
      some later measures of the Bach piece.

268   "Rhapsody in blue." Rhapsody in blue. 1977 Private
      Stock PS-2028, US.

      Source: Gershwin/Rhapsody in blue

269   "Romeo and Juliet." Walter Murphy's discosymphony.
      1979 N.Y. International BKL1-3506, US.

      Source: Tchaikovsky/Romeo and Juliet

270   "Russian dressing." A fifth of Beethoven. 1976
      Private Stock PS-2015, US.

      Source: Tchaikovsky/Piano concerto no. 1 in B flat
      minor, op. 23

271   "Toccata and funk in D minor." Phantom of the opera.
      1978 Private Stock PS-7010, US (album); 1978
      Private Stock 45196, US (single).

      Source: J. S. Bach/Toccata and fugue in D minor, BWV
      538

NEON PHILHARMONIC ORCHESTRA

272   Switched on classics. 1982 Alshire S-5385, US.

      Source: The classical music is arranged in disco
      medleys which include bits and pieces of Tchaikovsky/
      Romeo and Juliet, Swan lake adagio; Rimsky-Korsakov/
      Flight of the bumblebee; Gershwin/Rhapsody in blue;
      Sibelius; Rossini; Mozart/Aria from the marriage of
      Figaro; Grieg/Piano concerto in A minor; Bizet;
      Rachmaninoff; Bach; Gounod-Bach/Ave Maria; Beethoven/
      Moonlight sonata (mvt. 1), Symphony no. 9; Offenbach;
      Strauss II; Brahms; Dinicu/Hora staccato; Clarke;
      Handel/Hallelujah chorus; and Liszt/Liebestraum
      Note: The orchestra is arranged and conducted by
      William Motzing.

NERO AND THE GLADIATORS

273   "In the hall of the mountain king." 1961 Decca
      F-11367, UK (single).

      Source: Grieg/Peer Gynt suite no. 1, op. 46, mvt. 4
      (In the hall of the mountain king)
      Note: This instrumental reached #48 on the British
      charts.

NEW GENERATION

274 "Smokey Blue's away." 1968 Spark SRL-1007, UK
     (single).

     Source: Dvorak/Symphony no. 9 (old no. 5) in E
     minor, op. 95 (from the new world)
     Note: This single reached #38 on the British charts.

NEW LONDON CHORALE

275 Young Messiah. 1979 Myrrh MSB-6658, US/ 1979 RCA
     RCALP-3104, UK.

     Source: Handel/Messiah
     Note: This score from the stage and TV production
     includes: Comfort ye -- Every valley -- Who shall
     abide -- O thou that tellest -- Unto us a Child is
     born -- He shall feed his flock -- He was despised --
     How beautiful are the feet -- Hallelujah -- I know
     that my Redeemer liveth -- Finale (Hallelujah)

NEW WORLD ENSEMBLE

276 The baroque connection. 1982 Arrival Records PNU-
     5140, US.

     Source: The large number of short classical excerpts
     used in medley fashion precludes a complete listing
     here. The section titles are: The baroque connec-
     tion (The single) -- The adagio connection -- The
     gigue connection -- The fugue connection (Bach) --
     The Handel connection -- The Vivaldi connection --
     The Scarlatti connection -- The baroque connection
     (reprise). The conductor is Ettore Stratta.

NEW YORK ELECTRIC STRING ENSEMBLE

277 "Allegro." New York Electric String Ensemble. 1968
     Esp-Disk ESP-1063, US.

     Source: Corelli/Sonata in A major, op. 4, no. 3

278 "Allegro." Tapestry. 1970 Columbia CS-9992, US.

     Source: J. S. Bach/Sonata in G minor

279 "Aria I" and "Aria II." New York Electric String
     Ensemble. 1968 Esp-Disk ESP-1063, US.

     Source: Morley

280 "Bourée from the klavierbüchlein für Friedmann Bach."
     New York Electric String Ensemble. 1968 Esp-Disk
     ESP-1063, US.

Source: J. S. Bach/Klavierbüchlein für Friedemann Bach, Bourrée

281 "Fugue #2 from the well-tempered clavier." <u>New York Electric String Ensemble</u>. 1968 Esp-Disk ESP-1063, US.

Source: J. S. Bach/Well-tempered clavier, book I, fugue no. 2

282 "Gavotte from the third English suite." <u>New York Electric String Ensemble</u>. 1968 Esp-Disk ESP-1063, US.

Source: J. S. Bach/English suite no. 3 in G minor, Gavotte

283 "Largo." <u>New York Electric String Ensemble</u>. 1968 Esp-Disk ESP-1063, US.

Source: Corelli/Sonata in A major, op. 4, no. 3

284 "Minuet." <u>New York Electric String Ensemble</u>. 1968 Esp-Disk ESP-1063, US.

Source: Telemann/Eine kleine suite der tafelmusik, Minuet

285 "Minuet from the first harpsichord suite." <u>New York Electric String Ensemble</u>. 1968 Esp-Disk ESP-1063, US.

Source: Purcell/Harpsichord suite no. 1 in G, Minuet

286 "Minuet from the notenbüchlein für Anna-Magdalena Bach." <u>New York Electric String Ensemble</u>. 1968 Esp-Disk ESP-1063, US.

Source: J. S. Bach/Notebook for Anna Magdalena Bach, Minuet

287 "Minuet trio from the klavierbüchlein für Friedemann Bach." <u>New York Electric String Ensemble</u>. 1968 Esp-Disk ESP-1063, US.

Source: J. S. Bach/Klavierbüchlein für Friedemann Bach, Minuet trio

288 "Polonaise from the notenbüchlein für Anna-Magdalena Bach." <u>New York Electric String Ensemble</u>. 1968 Esp-Disk ESP-1063, US.

Source: J. S. Bach/Notebook for Anna Magdalena Bach, Polonaise

289 "Pomposo." <u>Tapestry</u>. 1970 Columbia CS-9992, US.

Source: Purcell/Sonata in D major

290 "Presto." Tapestry. 1970 Columbia CS-9992, US.

Source: Purcell/Sonata in D major

291 "Sarabande." New York Electric String Ensemble.
     1968 Esp-Disk ESP-1063, US.

Source: Telemann/Eine kleine suite der tafelmusik,
Sarabande

292 "Springtime." New York Electric String Ensemble.
     1968 Esp-Disk ESP-1063, US.

Source: Morley/Springtime

NEW YORK ROCK & ROLL ENSEMBLE

293 "Aria." Faithful friends. 1969 Atco SD33-294, US/
     1969 Atco 228-932, UK.

Source: Morley

294 "Brandenburg." Faithful friends. 1969 Atco SD33-
     294, US/ 1969 Atco 228-932, UK (albums); 1969 Atco
     45-6671, US (single).

Source: J. S. Bach/Brandenburg concerto no. 5 in D
major, BWV 1050, mvt. 1
Note: This piece also appears on the cassette Bach
rock: the New York Rock & Roll Ensemble blends
classical themes with rock (197? Center for Cassette
Studies 11940).

295 "Trio sonata no. 1 in C major (2nd mvt.) alla breva
     fugue." New York Rock & Roll Ensemble. 1968 Atco
     SD33-240, US.

Source: J. S. Bach/Trio sonata no. 1 in C major,
mvt. 2

296 "Trio sonata no. 2 in G major." Faithful friends.
     1969 Atco SD33-294, US/ 1969 Atco 228-932, UK.

Source: J. S. Bach/Trio sonata no. 2 in G major

297 "A whiter shade of pale." Freedomburger. 1972
     Columbia KC-31317, US/ 1972 CBS 64324, UK (albums);
     1972 Columbia 4-45574, US (single).

Source: J. S. Bach/Suite no. 3 in D major for
orchestra, BWV 1068, Air for the G string/Wachet auf,
BWV 140, no. 1 (Sleepers, awake)
Note: This is a version of Procol Harum's song (see
324). It also appears on Bach rock: the New York

Rock & Roll Ensemble blends classical themes with rock (197? Center for Cassette Studies 11940).

NICE

298   "Acceptance 'Brandenburger'." Ars longa vita brevis. 1969 Immediate Z12-52020, US/ 1968 Immediate IMSP-020, UK.

Source: J. S. Bach/Brandenburg concerto no. 3 in G major, BWV 1048
Note: This piece is the third movement of the Nice suite "Ars longa vita brevis." It also appears on Greatest hits (1977 Immediate IML-2003, UK). The album Ars longa vita brevis was reissued (1973 Columbia IMP-11634, US/ 1978 Charly CR-300019, UK). Band member Keith Emerson later joined Emerson, Lake & Palmer.

299   "America." Ars longa vita brevis. 1969 Immediate Z12-52020, US/ 1968 Immediate IMSP-020, UK (albums); 1968 Immediate 5008, US/ 1968 Immediate IM-068, UK (singles).

Source: Dvorak/Symphony no. 9 (old no. 5) in E minor (from the new world), op. 95, mvt. 4, 1st & 2nd theme
Note: The introduction and break added to the Bernstein/Sondheim tune are based on Dvorak. The song also appears on Elegy (1971 Mercury SR-61324, US/ 1971 Charisma CAS-1030, UK), Greatest Hits (1977 Immediate IML-2003, UK), Keith Emerson with the Nice (1972 Mercury SRM-2-6500, US), and Autumn to spring (1973 Charisma CAS-1, US/ 1972 Charisma CS-1, UK).

300   "Country pie/Brandenburg concerto no. 6." The five bridges. 1970 Mercury SR-61295, US/ 1970 Charisma CAS-1014, UK (albums); 1970 Mercury 73114, US (Nice single), 1972 Mercury 73272, US (Keith Emerson single).

Source: J. S. Bach/Brandenburg concerto no. 6 in B flat, BWV 1051
Note: This song interweaves a Bob Dylan song with the Bach piece. It also appears on Keith Emerson with the Nice (1972 Mercury SRM-2-6500, US).

301   "Intermezzo from the Karelia suite." Ars longa vita brevis. 1969 Immediate Z12-52020, US/ 1968 Immediate IMSP-020, UK.

Source: Sibelius/Karelia suite for orchestra, op. 11, Intermezzo
Note: This piece also appears on The five bridges (1970 Mercury SR-61295, US/ 1970 Charisma CAS-1014, UK), Greatest hits (1977 Immediate IML-2003, UK), and Keith Emerson with the Nice (1972 Mercury SRM-2-6500, US).

302   "Pathétique symphony no. 6, 3rd mvt." The five
        bridges. 1970 Mercury SR-61295, US/ 1970 Charisma
        CAS-1014, UK.

        Source: Tchaikovsky/Symphony no. 6 in B minor, op.
        74 (Pathétique), mvt. 3
        Note: This version was recorded with the Sinfonia of
        London (see 304 for a Nice only version). It also
        appears on Keith Emerson with the Nice (1972 Mercury
        SRM-2-6500, US).

303   "Rondo." The thoughts of Emerlist Davjack. 1967
        Immediate 52004, US/ 1967 Immediate IMSP-016, UK.

        Source: Mozart/Piano sonata no. 11 in A major, K.
        300i (331), mvt. 3 (Rondo alla turca)
        Note: This commonly asserted connection is somewhat
        misleading. The tune is actually that of Dave
        Brubeck's "Blue rondo a la turk" from 1960 which uses
        similar classical rondo form and Turkish folk rhythm,
        but not the actual tune of Mozart. The Nice version
        also appears on Greatest hits (1977 Immediate IML-
        2003, UK) and in a live version as "Rondo '69" on
        Nice (1970 Immediate Z12-52022, US/ 1969 Immediate
        IMSP-026, UK). The thoughts of Emerlist Davjack was
        reissued (1973 Columbia IMP-11633, US/ 1978 Charly
        CR-300021, UK). Nice was reissued (1973 Columbia
        IMP-11635, US/ 1978 Charly CR-300014, UK).

304   "3rd movement, Pathétique symphony." Elegy. 1971
        Mercury SR-61324, US/ 1971 Charisma CAS-1030, UK.

        Source: Tchaikovsky/Symphony no. 6 in B minor, op.
        74 (Pathétique), mvt. 3
        Note: This is the same piece as in entry 302, but
        without the orchestra. It also appears on Keith
        Emerson with the Nice (1972 Mercury SRM-2-6500), US).

NIMBLE, JACK B., AND THE QUICKS

305   "Nut rocker." 1962 Dot 45-16319, US (single).

        Source: Tchaikovsky/Nutcracker suite, op. 71a, March
        of the wooden soldiers
        See also B. Bumble and the Stingers

NITZSCHE, JACK

306   Chopin '66. 1966 Reprise R-6200, US.

        Source: Chopin/ as listed below
        Note: This album contains contemporary arrangements
        of Chopin themes listed as: Prelude #15 in D flat,
        op. 28 (Raindrop) -- Funeral procession -- Fantasie
        impromptu (op. 66) -- Revolutionary etude (Etude in C
        minor, op. 10, no. 12) -- Prelude #6 in D, op. 28 --

Etude in E (op. 10, no. 3) -- Prelude #1 in C, op. 28
-- Funeral march -- Prelude #4 in G -- Prelude #3 in
G, op. 28.

NOMI, KLAUS

307 "Samson and Delilah." Klaus Nomi. 1981 RCA RCALP-
     6026, UK (album); 1980 ? (single).

     Source: Saint-Saens/Samson and Delilah, op. 47, Aria
     Note: This is a new wave artist's version.

NYLONS

308 "Bumble boogie." One size fits all. 1982 Attic
     LAT-1152, Canada.

     Source: Rimsky-Korsakov/The legend of Tsar Saltan,
     first theme (Flight of the bumblebee)
     Note: This version uses harmonized vocals and
     percussion only. See also B. Bumble and the Stingers

PARKS, VAN DYKE

309 "Cannon in D." Clang of the Yankee Reaper. 1975
     Warner Bros. BS-2878, US/ 1975 Warner Bros. K-
     56161, UK.

     Source: Parks credits Pachelbel on the album,
     apparently referring to the "Canon in D". However,
     the tune is actually "Ein feste burg" by Martin
     Luther and also used by J. S. Bach in his cantata 80.
     Either an honest mistake in attribution and spelling
     was made, or it's all some sort of musical joke.

PHILARMONICS

310 "A la turka." The masters in Philadelphia. 1977
     Capricorn CPN-0179, US.

     Source: Mozart/Piano sonata no. 11 in A major, K.
     300i (331), mvt. 3 (Rondo alla turca)

311 "1812 overture." The masters in Philadelphia. 1977
     Capricorn CPN-0179, US.

     Source: Tchaikovsky/1812 overture, op. 49

312 "For Elise." The masters in Philadelphia. 1977
     Capricorn CPN-0179, US (album); 1977 Capricorn 268,
     US (single).

     Source: Beethoven/Für Elise
     Note: This disco instrumental single reached #100 on
     the Billboard pop singles chart.

313 "Lullaby." The masters in Philadelphia. 1977
     Capricorn CPN-0179, US.

     Source: Brahms/Lullaby (Cradle song)

314 "Piano concerto." The masters in Philadelphia. 1977
     Capricorn CPN-0179, US.

     Source: Tchaikovsky/Piano concerto no. 1 in B flat
     minor, op. 23

315 "Prince Igor 1st theme from polovetsian dance." The
     masters in Philadelphia. 1977 Capricorn CPN-0179,
     US.

     Source: Borodin/Polovetsian dances from Prince Igor,
     first theme

316 "Reverie." The masters in Philadelphia. 1977
     Capricorn CPN-0179, US.

     Source: Schumann/Scenes from childhood, op. 15,
     Träumerei (Reverie)

317 "Symphony number 5 from the new world." The masters
     in Philadelphia. 1977 Capricorn CPN-0179, US.

     Source: Dvorak/Symphony no. 9 (old no. 5) in E minor
     (from the new world), op. 95, mvt. 2

PHILHARMONIC 2000

318 Disconcerto. 1976 Phonogram 6308-277 (Philips
     6381-074), 198? Philips 7215-074, UK.

     Source: Information about this disco style album is
     scarce. The pieces included on it and some specula-
     tions as to the sources of some of them are: Swan
     song (Tchaikovsky/Swan lake?) -- G-string boogie
     (Bach/Air for the G string?) -- Paradise lost (?) --
     Hallelujah hustle (Handel/Hallelujah chorus?) --
     1912/76 (?) -- New world (Dvorak/New world symphony?)
     -- Disconcerto (?) -- Moonshine (Beethoven/Moonlight
     sonata?) -- Bee's knees (Rimsky-Korsakov/Flight of
     the bumblebee?) -- Song and dance (?) -- Big apple
     (?) -- Save our soul (?).

PILTDOWN MEN

319 "Piltdown rides again." Piltdown rides again.
     1960-61 Capitol EAP-1-20155 (EP); 1960 Capitol
     4460, US/ 1961 Capitol CL-15175, UK (singles).

     Source: Rossini/William Tell overture
     Note: This instrumental was recorded originally in
     the U.S.

PRESLEY, ELVIS

320   "Also sprach Zarathustra." <u>Elvis as recorded at
      Madison Square Garden</u>. 1972 RCA Victor LSP(AFL1)-
      4776, US/ 1972 RCA SF-8296, UK.

      Source: R. Strauss/Also sprach Zarathustra, op. 30
      Note: This concert introduction also appears on
      <u>Aloha from Hawaii via satellite</u> (1973 RCA VPSX-6089,
      CPD2-2642, US/ 1973 RCA DPS-2040, UK) and <u>Elvis in
      concert</u> (1977 RCA CPL2-2587, US).

321   "Am I ready." <u>Spinout</u>. 1966 RCA Victor LPM-3702
      (mono), LSP-3702 (stereo), US/ 1966 RCA RD-7820
      (mono), SF-7820 (stereo), UK (the UK album has the
      title <u>California holiday</u>).

      Source: MacDowell/Woodland sketches, op. 51, no. 1
      (To a wild rose)
      Note: This film soundtrack album was later reissued
      (1977 RCA AFL1-2560, 1980 RCA AYL1-3684, US). This
      song also appears on <u>Burning love and hits from his
      movies, vol. 2</u> (1972 RCA Camden CAS-2595, US).

322   "Tonight is so right for love." <u>G. I. blues</u>. 1960
      RCA Victor LPM-2256 (mono), LSP-2256 (stereo), US/
      1960 RCA RD-27192 (mono), SF-5078 (stereo), UK.

      Source: Offenbach/Tales of Hoffman, act II inter-
      mezzo (La barcarolle)
      Note: This film soundtrack album was later reissued
      (1977 RCA AFL1-2256, 1980 RCA AYL1-3735, US). This
      song also appears on <u>Burning love and hits from his
      movies, vol. 2</u> (1972 RCA Camden CAS-2595, US).

323   "Tonight's all right for love." <u>Elvis--a legendary
      performer, v. 1</u>. c1973, 1974 RCA Victor CPL-1-
      0341, US and UK.

      Source: J. Strauss/Tales from the Vienna woods, op.
      325
      Note: This is an alternate version of entry 322
      above. It was used in the 1960 European film version
      of <u>G. I. blues</u> and was previously unreleased in
      English-speaking countries until this compilation.
      The compilation was also released as a picture disc
      in 1978 (less than 12 copies) and reissued as a
      regular album in 1983.

PROCOL HARUM

324   "A whiter shade of pale." <u>Procol Harum</u>. 1967 Deram
      18008, US/ 1967 Regal Zonophone LRZ-1001, UK
      (albums); 1967 Deram 7507, US/ 1967 Deram DM-126,
      UK (singles).

      Source: J. S. Bach/Suite no. 3 in D major for
      orchestra, BWV 1068, Air for the G string/ Wachet
      auf, BWV 140, no. 1 (Sleepers, awake)

Note: This famous song is often attributed to either
of the Bach pieces above, however the band, itself,
lays claim to neither. The tune is closest to the
first, but contains some elements of both. The U.S.
single reached #5 on the Billboard pop singles chart;
the British single reached #1 on their charts and won
a 1967/68 Novello Award. Procol Harum was reissued
as A whiter shade of pale (197? A&M SP-4373, US).
The singles were reissued (1972 A&M 1389, US/ 1972
Magnifly Echo 10, UK). The song is also included on
Best of Procol Harum (1972 A&M SP-4401 [3529], US).
Some other major versions were recorded by Munich
Machine (see 254) and New York Rock & Roll Ensemble
(see 297). Some minor versions were recorded by the
Dells (1971 Cadet 5679, US, B-side of the single "The
glory of love"; also on album Love is blue 1969 Cadet
LPS-829, US), the Hesitations (1968 Kapp 948, US,
single), Joe Cocker (Luxury you can afford 1978
Elektra/Asylum 6E-145, US), and HSAS (Through the
fire 1984 Geffen GHS-4023, US).

QUATRO, MICHAEL (MIKE)

324A "Adagio." Dancers, romancers, dreamers & schemers.
      1976 United Artists UA-LA587-G, Prodigal P6-
      10010S1, US/ 1976 Prodigal PDL-2001, UK.

      Source: Albinoni/Adagio in G minor

325   "Ave rock Maria." In collaboration with the gods.
      1975 United Artists UA-LA420-G, US/ 1975 United
      Artists UAS-29785, UK.

      Source: J. S. Bach; Gounod/Ave Maria

326   "Prelude in A^b crazy (classical variations)." Look
      deeply into the mirror. 1973 Evolution 3021, US.

      Source: ?
      Note: This possible classical theme could not be
      verified. It appears as "Prelude in A^b crazy II" on
      In collaboration with the gods (see 325).

327   "Pure Chopin." Dancers, romancers, dreamers &
      schemers. 1976 United Artists UA-LA587-G, Prodigal
      P6-10010S1, US/ 1976 Prodigal PDL-2001, UK (al-
      bums); 1976 Prodigal 631, US (single).

      Source: Chopin/Nocturne in E flat major, op. 9,
      no. 2

328   "Rachmaninoff's prelude." Paintings. 1972 Evolution
      3011, US.

      Source: Rachmaninoff/Prelude in C sharp minor, op.
      3, no. 2

329   "Rockmaninoff's prelude in C blunt funk." In col-
        laboration with the gods. 1975 United Artists
        UA-LA420-G, US/ 1975 United Artists UAS-29785, UK.

        Source: Rachmaninoff/Prelude in C sharp minor, op.
        3, no. 2

330   "Rollerbach (Disko-Bach)." Dancers, romancers,
        dreamers & schemers. 1976 United Artists
        UA-LA587-G, Prodigal P6-10010S1, US/ 1976 Prodigal
        PDL-2001, UK.

        Source: J. S. Bach/Toccata and fugue in D minor, BWV
        538

RABBITT

331   "Schumann." A croak & a grunt in the night. 1977
        Capricorn CP-0190, US.

        Source: Schumann

RAIDERS. See REVERE, PAUL, AND THE RAIDERS

RAINBOW

332   "Difficult to cure (Beethoven's ninth)." Difficult
        to cure. 1981 Polydor PD-1-6316, US/ 1981 Polydor
        POLD-5036, UK.

        Source: Beethoven/Symphony no. 9 in D minor, op.
        125, mvt. 4, first theme
        Note: This group is sometimes known as Ritchie
        Blackmore's Rainbow. Ritchie Blackmore is associated
        with the rock group Deep Purple.

RENAISSANCE

333   "At the harbour." Ashes are burning. 1973 Capitol
        ST-11216, US/ 1973 Sovereign 7261, UK.

        Source: Debussy/Preludes, book 1, no. 10 (The
        engulfed cathedral), second theme
        Note: The piano solo at the beginning and conclusion
        of the song is based on the Debussy piece. The song
        also appears on In the beginning (197? Capitol
        SWBC-11871, US), and in a live version on Live at
        Carnegie Hall (1976 Sire SASY-3902 [6029], US/ 1976
        BTM 2001, UK).

        "Mother Russia" and "Song of Scheherazade" are only
        inspired by, not based on, Shostakovich and
        Rimsky-Korsakov, respectively. Therefore, they will
        not be included in this section (see 804 and 626).

RENAISSANCE ORCHESTRA

334   Classics '72. 1972 Sunset SLS-50284, UK.

        Source: Bizet, Chopin, Handel, Bach, Grieg, Mozart,
        Tchaikovsky, Beethoven, and Dvorak

Note: The orchestra is augmented by a pop rhythm
section. The music was arranged and produced by
Irving Martin.

REVERE, PAUL, AND THE RAIDERS

335 "Like long hair." Like long hair. 1961 Gardena
     G-1000, US (album); 1961 Gardena 116, US (single).

     Source: Rachmaninoff/Prelude in A major
     Note: This instrumental reached #38 on the Billboard
     pop singles chart. It is included on the bootleg
     album Rarities (19?? D-539).

RIOS, MIGUEL

336 "A song of joy." A song of joy. 1970 A&M SP-4267,
     US (album); 1970 A&M 1193, US/ 1970 A&M AMS-790, UK
     (singles).

     Source: Beethoven/Symphony no. 9 in D minor, op.
     125, mvt. 4, first theme
     Note: The very first appearance of this song was
     actually a 1969 Spanish single on the Hispavox label
     entitled "Himno a la alegria." The orchestra was
     conducted by Waldo de los Rios. The U.S. single
     reached #14 on the Billboard pop singles chart.

RIOS, WALDO DE LOS

337 Mozartmania. 1971 United Artists UAS-5554, US/ 1971
     A&M AMLS-68066, UK (the UK album has the title
     Mozart in the seventies).

     Source: Mozart/as listed below
     Note: The Manuel de Falla Orchestra, arranged and
     conducted by Waldo de los Rios, and its modern rhythm
     section perform: Mozart's 13th (Serenade no. 13 in G
     major) -- What is love (Aria from marriage of Figaro)
     -- Overture 492 (Marriage of Figaro) -- Mozart 21
     (Concerto no. 21 for piano and orchestra in C major,
     2nd mvt.) -- Musical charade (Musikalischer spass,
     4th tempo) -- Mozart nova (Variations on dear harmony
     from the magic flute).

338 Operas. 1974 Warner Bros. BS-2801, US.

     Source: excerpts from Verdi/Aida, La traviata,
     Nabucco, Rigoletto; Donizetti/Elixir de amor;
     Rossini/Barber of Seville; Puccini/Madame Butterfly;
     Wagner/Tannhauser

339 Sinfonias. 1971 United Artists UAS-6802, US.

     Source: Pieces are listed on the album with their
     correct classical titles as follows: Beethoven.
     Ninth symphony in D minor, choral 4th mvt., "Ode to
     joy" -- Schubert. Eighth symphony in C minor,

"Incomplete," 1st mvt. -- Mozart. Symphony no. 40 in G minor K. 550, 1st mvt. (Allegro molto) -- Brahms. Third symphony in F major, 3rd mvt. -- Dvorak. Symphony no. 9, op. 95, "New world," 4th mvt. (Allegro con fuoco)/2nd mvt. (Largo) -- Haydn. Symphony of the toys in C major, 2nd mvt. -- Tchaikovsky. Symphony no. 5 in E minor, 2nd mvt. -- Mendelssohn. Fourth symphony in A major, "Italian," 1st mvt.
Note: The album reached #53 on the Billboard pop album chart. A single was released for "Mozart symphony #40 in G minor" (1971 United Artists 7468, US/ 1971 A&M AMS-836, UK) which reached #67 on the Billboard pop singles chart.

340   Symphonies for the '70s. 1974 Warner Bros. BS-2874, US.

Source: Brahms, Beethoven, Mendelssohn, Berlioz, Tchaikovsky, Haydn, Lalo

ROCHES

341   "The hallelujah chorus." Keep on doing. 1982 Warner Bros. 1-23725, US/ 1982 Warner Bros. K-57027, UK.

Source: Handel/Messiah, Hallelujah chorus
Note: This trio of sisters usually sings folk rock. They sing this song a cappella.

ROLLING STONES

342   "Intro." Love you live. 1977 Rolling Stones COC-2-9001, US/ 1977 Rolling Stones COC-89101, UK.

Source: Copland/Fanfare for the common man
Note: This is actually a taped orchestra used as an introduction to the Rolling Stones concert.

ROTO ROOTER GOOD TIME CHRISTMAS BAND

343   "Fanfare/Buick LeSabre dance." The Roto Rooter Good Time Christmas Band. 1974 Vanguard VSD-79347, US.

Source: Khatchaturian/Gayne ballet, Sabre dance

344   "Hungarian dance no. 5." The Roto Rooter Good. Time Christmas Band. 1974 Vanguard VSD-79347, US.

Source: Brahms/Hungarian dance no. 5 in F sharp minor

345   "Overture and rite of spring." The Roto Rooter Good Time Christmas Band. 1974 Vanguard VSD-79347, US.

Source: Stravinsky/Rite of spring

346   "Swamp lake." The Roto Rooter Good Time Christmas Band. 1974 Vanguard VSD-79347, US.

Source: Tchaikovsky/Swan lake, suite from the
ballet, op. 20a

ROYAL PHILHARMONIC ORCHESTRA

347   Hooked on classics: the album.   1981 RCA AFL1-4194,
         US/ 1981 K-tel ONE-1146, UK.

      Source: This album uses very short fragments of 106
      classical themes--too numerous to list here.
      Note: The orchestra arrangements include a prominent
      disco beat and were conducted by Louis Clark. The
      titles of the separate sections are: Hooked on
      classics parts 1 and 2 -- Hooked on romance -- Hooked
      on classics part 3 -- Hooked on Bach -- Hooked on
      Tchaikovsky -- Hooked on a song -- Hooked on Mozart
      -- Hooked on Mendelssohn -- Hooked on a can can. The
      album made the top ten and the single of "Hooked on
      classics" (1981 RCA 12304, US) reached #10 on the
      Billboard pop singles chart. Another single was
      released as "Hooked on romance/Hooked on Tchaikovsky"
      (1982 RCA 13037, US).

348   Hooked on classics II: can't stop the classics.
         1982 RCA AFL1-4373, US.

      Source: This album uses 98 separate classical
      fragments--too numerous to mention here.
      Note: The Royal Choral Society also appears on this
      album. Louis Clark conducts the orchestra and
      chorus. The section titles are: Can't stop the
      classics -- Hooked on America -- Hooked on romance
      (pt. 2) -- Can't stop the classics (pt. 2) -- A night
      at the opera -- Tales of the Vienna waltz (J.
      Strauss) -- Hooked on baroque -- If you knew Sousa --
      If you knew Sousa (and friends).

349   Hooked on classics III: journey through the clas-
         sics. 1983 RCA AFL1-4588, US.

      Source: This album consists of numerous short
      classical fragments too numerous to list.
      Note: The sections, conducted by Louis Clark, are
      entitled: Also sprach Zarathustra -- Journey through
      the classics -- Hooked on Haydn -- Hooked on romance
      (opus 3) -- Viva Vivaldi -- Dance of the furies --
      Scotland the brave (Hookery jiggery jock) -- Journey
      through the classics (part 2) -- Journey through
      America -- Hooked on marching -- Symphony of the seas
      -- Hooked on Rodgers and Hammerstein.

SRC

350   "In the hall of the mountain king/Bolero." Mile-
         stones. 1969 Capitol ST-134, US.

Source: Grieg/Peer Gynt suite no. 1, op. 46, mvt. 4
(In the hall of the mountain king); Ravel/Bolero

SECOND CITY SOUND

351 "Tchaikovsky one." 1966 Decca F-12310, UK (single).

Source: Tchaikovsky/Piano concerto no. 1 in B flat
minor, op. 23
Note: This instrumental reached #22 on the British
charts.

SHIRE, DAVID

352 "Night on disco mountain." Saturday night fever.
1977 RSO RS-2-4001, US.

Source: Moussorgsky/Night on bald mountain
Note: This disco piece is on the film soundtrack
album.

SIMON, PAUL

353 "American tune." There goes rhymin' Simon. 1973
Columbia PC(KC)-32280, US/ 1973 CBS 69035, UK
(albums); 1973 Columbia 45900, US (single).

Source: J. S. Bach/St. Matthew passion, BWV 63,
O sacred Head (also known as: O Thou with hate
surrounded; O Head, all scarred and bleeding; O Haupt
voll blut und wunden)
Note: The single reached #35 on the Billboard pop
singles chart. The song also appears on Paul Simon
in concert, live rhymin' (1974 Columbia PC-32855, US/
1974 CBS 69059, UK) and Greatest hits, etc. (1977
Columbia JC-35032, US/ 1977 CBS 86047, UK).

SKY

354 "Andante." Sky. 1980 Arista A2L-8302, US/ 1980
Ariola AD-SKY2, UK (the UK album has title Sky 2).

Source: Vivaldi/Concert in G for 2 mandolins, mvt. 2

355 "Ballet-volta." Sky. 1980 Arista A2L-8302, US/ 1980
Ariola AD-SKY2, UK (the UK album has title Sky 2).

Source: Praetorius/Terpsichore (1612)

356 "Fantasy." Sky 4--forthcoming. 1982 Arista AL-9604,
US/ 1982 Ariola AD-SKY4, UK.

Source: Bach/Fantasy in C minor

357 "Gavotte and variations." Sky. 1980 Arista A2L-
8302, US/ 1980 Ariola AD-SKY2, UK (the UK album has
title Sky 2).

Source: Rameau/Simple and doubles

358   "Gymnopédie no. 1." Sky. 1979 Ariola ARLH-5022, UK.

Source: Satie/Gymnopédie no. 1

359   "March to the scaffold." Sky 4--forthcoming. 1982
      Arista AL-9604, US/ 1982 Ariola AD-SKY4, UK.

Source: Berlioz/Symphonie fantastique, op. 14, mvt.
4, first theme (March to the scaffold)

360   "Masquerade." Sky 4--forthcoming. 1982 Arista
      AL-9604, US/ 1982 Ariola AD-SKY4, UK.

Source: Khatchaturian/Incidental music for the play
"Maskerad" by Lermontov

361   "Ride of the Valkyries." Sky 4--forthcoming. 1982
      Arista AL-9604, US/ 1982 Ariola AD-SKY4, UK.

Source: Wagner/Der ring des Nibelungen, Die Walküre,
Ride of the Valkyries

362   "Sarabande." Sky 3. 1981 Arista AB-4288, US/ 1981
      Ariola AD-SKY3, UK.

Source: Handel/Suite no. 4 in D minor (from 2nd set
of piano suites), mvt. 3, Sarabande

363   "The swan." Sky 5--live. 1983 Ariola 302-171, UK.

Source: Saint-Saens/Carnaval des animaux, The swan

364   "Toccata." Sky. 1980 Arista A2L-8302, US/ 1980
      Ariola AD-SKY2, UK (the UK album has title Sky 2)
      (albums); 1981 Arista 568, US/ 1980 Ariola ARO-
      300, UK (singles).

Source: J. S. Bach/Toccata and fugue in D minor, BWV
538
Note: The U.S. single reached #83 on the Billboard
pop singles chart.

365   "Vivaldi." Sky. 1980 Arista A2L-8302, US/1980
      Ariola AD-SKY2, UK (the UK album has title Sky 2).

Source: Vivaldi?
Note: This piece may be only imitation Vivaldi. It
is credited to Darryl Way of Curved Air, but cer-
tainly sounds like Vivaldi. See also Curved Air

366   "Waltz no. 2." Sky 4--forthcoming. 1982 Arista
      AL-9604, US/ 1982 Ariola AD-SKY4, UK.

Source: Ravel/Valses nobles et sentimentales, no. 2

SLOCUM, BRAD

367 Sonic synsations. 1977 B. A. Slocum Records.

Source: as listed below
Note: These pieces, performed on ARP2600 synthesizer, are faithful to the classical originals as
listed on the album: Frederic Chopin/Etude number 18
in G-sharp minor, op. 25, no. 6 -- Frederic Chopin/
Etude number 3 in E major, op. 10, no. 3 -- J. S.
Bach/Prelude and fugue number 21 in B-flat major --
J. S. Bach/Air on G string -- J. S. Bach/Brandenburg
concerto number 2 in F major.

STARCASTLE

368 "Lady of the lake." Starcastle. 1976 Epic PE-33914,
US/ 1976 Epic 81347, UK (albums); 1976 Epic 8-
50226, US (single).

Source: Stravinsky/Firebird suite

STORM, BILLY

369 "I've come of age." 1959 Columbia 41356, US
(single).

Source: Tchaikovsky/Symphony no. 5 in E minor, op.
64, mvt. 2, second theme
Note: This single reached #28 on the Billboard pop
singles chart.

STRATTA, ETTORE. See BAROQUE POPS and NEW WORLD ENSEMBLE

STYX

370 "Clair de lune/Ballerina." Crystal ball. 1976 A&M
SP-4604, US/ 1976 A&M AMLH-64604, UK.

Source: Debussy/Suite bergamasque, Clair de lune,
first theme
Note: The piano introduction to this song is the
Debussy piece.

371 "Fanfare for the common man." Styx. 1972 Wooden
Nickel WNS(BXLI)-1008, US.

Source: Copland/Fanfare for the common man
Note: Copland's theme is only very loosely used as a
source for the "Fanfare" section of the larger piece
entitled "Movement for the common man." The album
has been reissued twice and retitled Styx I (1980 RCA
AFL1-3593, 1981 RCA AYL1-3888, US).

372 "Hallelujah chorus (from Handel's Messiah)." The
serpent is rising. 1973 Wooden Nickel SWL1(BXLI)-
0287, US.

Source: Handel/Messiah, Hallelujah chorus
Note: The album was reissued under the title <u>Serpent</u>
(1980 RCA AFL1-3595, 1981 AYL1-4111, US).

373 "Little fugue in G." <u>Styx II</u>. 1973 Wooden Nickel
    WNS(BXLI)-1012, US.

Source: J. S. Bach/Fugue in G minor, BWV 578 (Little
fugue in G minor)
Note: The album was retitled <u>Lady</u> and reissued (197?
RCA AFL1-3111, 1980 RCA AFL1-3594, 1982 RCA AYL1-
4233, US).

SUPREMES

374 "Joy to the world." <u>Merry Christmas</u>. 1965 Motown
    MS-638, US.

Source: Handel/Messiah, Hallelujah chorus
Note: The first few measures of Handel's theme are
used at the beginning and in a later part of "Joy to
the world," a Christmas carol. The song also appears
on <u>A Motown Christmas</u> (1973 Motown M-795V2, 1978
Motown 5256ML2, US). <u>Merry Christmas</u> was reissued
later (1978 Motown 5252ML, US).

375 "A lover's concerto." <u>I hear a symphony</u>. 1966
    Motown MS-643, US/ 1966 Tamla STML-11028, UK.

Source: J. S. Bach/Notebook for Anna Magdalena Bach,
Minuet in G
Note: This is a version of the song originally done
by the Toys (see 419). The Supremes' album was
reissued (1982 Motown M5-147V1, US).

376 "Stranger in paradise." <u>I hear a symphony</u>. 1966
    Motown MS-643, US/ 1966 Tamla STML-11028, UK.

Source: Borodin/Polovetsian dances from Prince Igor,
first theme
Note: This song has also been done by non-rock
musicians. The Supremes' album was reissued (1982
Motown M5-147V1, US).

SYNTHESCOPE DIGITAL SYNTHESIZER ENSEMBLE

377 <u>The electronic Messiah</u>. 1982 MMG (Moss Music Group)
    D-MMG-113, US.

Source: Handel/Messiah
Note: This digital recording combines the cathedral-
recorded voices of the Elmer Iseler Singers with
synthesizer tracks created by the Synthescope. The
contents are: Sinfonia (Overture) -- And the glory
of the Lord -- For unto us a Child is born -- Pifa
(Pastoral symphony) -- Glory to God -- Behold the

Lamb of God -- Surely He hath borne our griefs -- And
with His stripes -- All we like sheep -- Hallelujah
-- Worthy is the Lamb -- Blessing and honour -- Amen.

TAK TIKS

378 "Nut rocker." 1965 Guyden 2130, US (single).

Source: Tchaikovsky/Nutcracker suite, op. 71a, March
of the wooden soldiers
See also B. Bumble and the Stingers

TELL, WILLIE, AND THE OVERTURES

379 "The soul ranger." 1969 Chess 2086, US (single).

Source: Rossini/William Tell overture (also used as
Lone Ranger theme)

TEMPLE CITY KAZOO ORCHESTRA

380 "Kazooed on klassics." 1982 Rhino RNOR-016, US
     (single).

Source: medley of themes from Beethoven/Symphony no.
5 in C minor, op. 67, mvt. 1, first theme; Rimsky-
Korsakov/The legend of Tsar Saltan, first theme
(Flight of the bumblebee); Tchaikovsky/Nutcracker
suite, op. 71a, March of the wooden soldiers;
Rossini/William Tell overture; Offenbach/Orpheus in
the underworld, act I, Galop, second theme; Handel/
Messiah, Hallelujah chorus; Wagner/Der ring des
Nibelungen, Die Walküre, Ride of the Valkyries;
Brahms/Hungarian dance no. 5 in F sharp minor, first
theme
Note: Kazoos with a disco beat, supplied by hand
claps, parody "Hooked on classics" (see 347). The
kazoo single also appears on the album The Rhino
Brothers present the world's worst records (1983
Rhino RNLP-809, US).

381 "2001 sprach kazoostra." Some kazoos. 1978 Rhino
     RNEP-501, US (EP).

Source: R. Strauss/Also sprach Zarathustra, op. 30

TITANS

382 "Tchaikovsky rides again." 1963 Soma 1402, US
     (single).

Source: Tchaikovsky
Note: This is the B-side of the single "Summer
place."

TOMITA (Isao Tomita)

383 "Arabesque no. 1." Snowflakes are dancing. 1974 RCA
     Red Seal ARL1-0488, US (album); 1974 RCA PB-10083,
     US (single).

     Source: Debussy/Arabesque no. 1 in E
     Note: The album Snowflakes are dancing, performed on
     synthesizer, reached #57 on the Billboard pop album
     chart. It was nominated in 1974 in the Grammy
     categories of classical album of the year, classical
     performance by instrumental soloist without orches-
     tra, and best engineered classical recording.

384 "Aranjuez." Kosmos. 1978 RCA Red Seal ARL1-2616,
     US/1978 RCA RL-42652, UK.

     Source: Rodrigo/Concierto de Aranjuez, Adagio

385 "Bolero." Bolero. c1979, 1980 RCA Red Seal ARL1-
     3412, US.

     Source: Ravel/Bolero
     Note: This synthesizer piece also appears on
     Tomita's A voyage through his greatest hits, vol. 2
     (1981 RCA Red Seal ARL1-4019, US).

386 "Clair de lune." Snowflakes are dancing. 1974 RCA
     Red Seal ARL1-0488, US (album); 1974 RCA APBO-0308,
     US (single).

     Source: Debussy/Suite bergamasque, Clair de lune
     Note: This synthesizer piece also appears on
     Tomita's greatest hits (1979 RCA Red Seal ARL1-3439,
     US/ 1979 RCA RL-43076, 1981 RCA RCALP-3037, UK).

387 "Daphnis and Chloe, suite no. 2." Bolero. c1979,
     1980 RCA Red Seal ARL1-3412, US.

     Source: Ravel/Daphnis and Chloe, suite no. 2
     Note: Sections are entitled "Day break," "Panto-
     mime," and "General dance."

388 "Dawn over the triangle and mysterious electric
     waves." The Bermuda Triangle. 1979 RCA Red Seal
     ARL1-2885, US/ 1979 RCA RL-12885, UK.

     Source: Prokofiev/Symphony no. 6 in E flat minor,
     op. 111, mvt. 1
     Note: The album The Bermuda Triangle received a
     Grammy nomination in 1979 in the category of best
     engineered classical recording.

389 "The dazzling cylinder that crashed in Tunguska,
     Siberia." The Bermuda Triangle. 1979 RCA Red Seal
     ARL1-2885, US/ 1979 RCA RL-12885, UK.

Source: Prokofiev/Symphony no. 6 in E flat minor,
op. 111, mvt. 1
Note: This piece also is included on Tomita's <u>A</u>
<u>voyage through his greatest hits, vol. 2</u> (1981 RCA
Red Seal ARL1-4019, US).

390   "Electromagnetic waves descend." <u>The Bermuda</u>
      <u>Triangle</u>. 1979 RCA Red Seal ARL1-2885, US/ 1979
      RCA RL-12885, UK.

Source: Prokofiev/Romeo and Juliet, op. 64, suite
no. 2

391   "The engulfed cathedral." <u>Snowflakes are dancing</u>.
      1974 RCA Red Seal ARL1-0488, US.

Source: Debussy/Preludes, book 1, no. 10 (The
engulfed cathedral)

392   "Firebird." <u>Firebird</u>. 1976 RCA Red Seal ARL1-1312,
      US.

Source: Stravinsky/Firebird
Note: The sections included on the album are:
Introduction and dance of the firebird -- Round of
the princesses -- Infernal dance of King Kastchei --
Berceuse and finale. The album reached #71 on the
Billboard pop album chart. "Firebird: infernal
dance" appears on <u>Tomita's greatest hits</u> (1979 RCA
Red Seal ARL1-3439, US/ 1979 RCA RL-43076, 1981 RCA
RCALP-3037, UK) and "Firebird suite: finale" appears
on <u>A voyage through his greatest hits, vol. 2</u> (1981
RCA Red Seal ARL1-4019, US).

393   "Footprints on the snow." <u>Snowflakes are dancing</u>.
      1974 RCA Red Seal ARL1-0488, US.

Source: Debussy/Preludes, book 1, no. 6

394   "Gardens in the rain." <u>Snowflakes are dancing</u>. 1974
      RCA Red Seal ARL1-0488, US.

Source: Debussy/Estampes no. 3 (Gardens in the rain)

395   "The giant pyramid and its ancient people." <u>The</u>
      <u>Bermuda Triangle</u>. 1979 RCA Red Seal ARL1-2885, US/
      1979 RCA RL-12885, UK.

Source: Prokofiev/Scythian suite, op. 20

396   "The girl with the flaxen hair." <u>Snowflakes are</u>
      <u>dancing</u>. 1974 RCA Red Seal ARL1-0488, US.

Source: Debussy/Preludes, book 1, no. 8 (The girl
with the flaxen hair)
Note: This piece is also included on <u>A voyage</u>

through his greatest hits, vol. 2 (1981 RCA Red Seal
ARL1-4019, US).

397   "Golliwog's cakewalk." Snowflakes are dancing.   1974
        RCA Red Seal ARL1-0488, US (album); 1974 RCA
        APBO-0308, US (single).

      Source: Debussy/Children's corner no. 6
      Note: This also appears on Tomita's greatest hits
      (1979 RCA Red Seal ARL1-3439, US/ 1979 RCA RL-43076,
      1981 RCA RCALP-3037, UK).

398   Grand Canyon.   1982 RCA Red Seal ARL1-4317, US/ 1982
        RCA RS-9005, UK.

      Source: Grofé/Grand Canyon suite
      Note: The Plasma Symphony Orchestra of electronic
      instruments performs sections entitled: Sunrise --
      Painted desert -- On the trail -- Sunset -- Cloud-
      burst.

399   "The harp of the ancient people with songs of Venus
        and space children." The Bermuda Triangle.   1979
        RCA Red Seal ARL1-2885, US/ 1979 RCA RL-12885, UK.

      Source: Prokofiev/Violin concerto no. 1, op. 19,
      mvt. 3

400   "Hora staccato." Kosmos.   1978 RCA Red Seal ARL1-
        2616, US/ 1978 RCA RL-42652, UK.

      Source: Dinicu; Heifetz/Hora staccato
      Note: This also appears on Tomita's greatest hits
      (1979 RCA Red Seal ARL1-3439, US/ 1979 RCA RL-43076,
      1981 RCA RCALP-3037, UK).

401   "Mother Goose suite." Bolero.   c1979, 1980 RCA Red
        Seal ARL1-3412, US.

      Source: Ravel/Mother Goose suite
      Note: The sections of the suite are entitled: Pavan
      of the sleeping beauty -- Hop-o'-my-thumb --
      Laideronette, empress of the pagodas -- Conversations
      of beauty and the beast -- The fairy garden.

402   "A night on bare mountain." Firebird.   1976 RCA Red
        Seal ARL1-1312, US.

      Source: Moussorgsky/Night on bald mountain

403   "Pacific 231." Kosmos.   1978 RCA Red Seal ARL1-2616,
        US/ 1978 RCA RL-42652, UK.

      Source: Honegger/Pacific 231
      Note: This also appears on A voyage through his
      greatest hits, vol. 2 (1981 RCA Red Seal ARL1-4019,
      US).

404   "Passepied." Snowflakes are dancing. 1974 RCA Red
      Seal ARL1-0488, US.

      Source: Debussy/Suite bergamasque, Passepied
      Note: This also appears on A voyage through his
      greatest hits, vol. 2 (1981 RCA Red Seal ARL1-4019,
      US).

405   "Pavan for a dead princess." Bolero. c1979, 1980
      RCA Red Seal ARL1-3412, US.

      Source: Ravel/Pavan for a dead princess

406   "Peer Gynt: Solvejg's song." Kosmos. 1978 RCA Red
      Seal ARL1-2616, US/ 1978 RCA RL-42652, UK.

      Source: Grieg/Peer Gynt suite no. 2, op. 55, mvt. 4

407   Pictures at an exhibition. 1975 RCA Red Seal ARL1-
      0838, US.

      Source: Moussorgsky; Ravel/Pictures at an exhibition
      Note: This album reached #49 on the Billboard pop
      album chart. "Pictures at an exhibition: the hut on
      fowls' legs; the ballet of the chicks in their
      shells" also appears on A voyage through his greatest
      hits, vol. 2 (1981 RCA Red Seal ARL1-4019, US).
      "Great gate of Kiev" also appears on Tomita's great-
      est hits (1979 RCA Red Seal ARL1-3439, US/ 1979 RCA
      RL-43076, 1981 RCA RCALP-3037, UK).

408   The planets. 1976 RCA Red Seal ARL1-1919, US/ 1977
      RCA RL-11919, UK.

      Source: Holst/The planets, op. 32
      Note: This album was banned in the U.K. in 1977
      after Holst's daughter won a court injunction. She
      objected to the synthesizer version of her father's
      work. The sections are entitled: Mars (the bringer
      of war) -- Venus (the bringer of peace) --Mercury
      (the winged messenger) -- Jupiter (the bringer of
      jollity) -- Saturn (the bringer of old age) --
      Uranus (the magician) -- Neptune (the mystic). A
      single "Mars/Venus" was released (1976 RCA PB-10819,
      US). "Mars" appears on Tomita's greatest hits (1979
      RCA Red Seal ARL1-3439, US/ 1979 RCA RL-43076, 1981
      RCA RCALP-3037, UK). "Venus" and "Mercury" appear on
      A voyage through his greatest hits, vol. 2 (1981 RCA
      Red Seal ARL1-4019, US).

409   "Prelude to afternoon of a faun." Firebird. 1976
      RCA Red Seal ARL1-1312, US.

      Source: Debussy/Prelude to afternoon of a faun

410   "Reverie." Snowflakes are dancing. 1974 RCA Red
      Seal ARL1-0488, US.

Source: Debussy/Reverie
Note: This also appears on A voyage through his greatest hits, vol. 2 (1981 RCA Red Seal ARL1-4019, US).

411   "The sea named 'Solaris'." Kosmos. 1978 RCA Red Seal ARL1-2616, US/ 1978 RCA RL-42652, UK.

Source: J. S. Bach/Three-part invention no. 2 in C minor, BWV 788; Ich ruf' zu dir, Herr Jesu Christ, BWV 639
Note: This piece also appears on A voyage through his greatest hits, vol. 2 (1981 RCA Red Seal ARL1-4019, US) and on the TV soundtrack album Music of Cosmos (1981 RCA ABL1-4003, US).

412   "Snowflakes are dancing." Snowflakes are dancing. 1974 RCA Red Seal ARL1-0488, US (album); 1974 RCA PB-10083, US (single).

Source: Debussy/Children's corner no. 4

413   "The song of Venus." The Bermuda Triangle. 1979 RCA Red Seal ARL1-2885, US/ 1979 RCA RL-12885, UK.

Source: Prokofiev/Violin concerto no. 1, op. 19, mvt. 1

414   "Space children in the underground kingdom called Agharta." The Bermuda Triangle. 1979 RCA Red Seal ARL1-2885, US/ 1979 RCA RL-12885, UK.

Source: Prokofiev/Symphony no. 5 in B flat major, op. 100, mvt. 2
Note: This appears as "Prokofiev symphony no. 5, 2nd mvt." on Tomita's greatest hits (1979 RCA Red Seal ARL1-3439, US/ 1979 RCA RL-43076, 1981 RCA RCALP-3037, UK).

415   "Space fantasy." Kosmos. 1978 RCA Red Seal ARL1-2616, US/ 1978 RCA RL-42652, UK.

Source: medley of themes from R. Strauss/Also sprach Zarathustra, op. 30; Wagner/Der ring des Nibelungen, Die Walküre, Ride of the Valkyries; Wagner/ Tannhäuser, overture
Note: This also appears on Tomita's greatest hits (1979 RCA Red Seal ARL1-3439, US/1979 RCA RL-43076, 1981 RCA RCALP-3037, UK).

416   "The unanswered question." Kosmos. 1978 RCA Red Seal ARL1-2616, US/ 1978 RCA RL-42652, UK.

Source: Ives/The unanswered question

417 "The visionary flight to the 1448 nebular group of
     the bootes." The Bermuda Triangle. 1979 RCA Red
     Seal ARL1-2885, US/ 1979 RCA RL-12885, UK.

     Source: Prokofiev/Scythian suite, op. 20

418 "A world of different dimensions." The Bermuda
     Triangle. 1979 RCA Red Seal ARL1-2885, US/ 1979
     RCA RL-12885, UK.

     Source: Sibelius/Valse triste

TOYS

419 "A lover's concerto." The Toys sing A lover's
     concerto and Attack. 1966 Dynovoice 9002, US
     (album); 1965 Dynovoice 209, US/ 1965 Stateside
     SS-460, UK (singles).

     Source: J. S. Bach/Notebook for Anna Magdalena Bach,
     Minuet in G
     Note: The single reached #2 on the Billboard pop
     singles chart and was an RIAA certified million
     seller. See also Supremes; Vogues

TRASHMEN

420 "Malagueña." Surfin' bird. 1964 Soma LPGA-200, US.

     Source: Albeniz; Lecuona/Malagueña

TRINITY. See AUGER, BRIAN, AND THE TRINITY

TRIUMVIRAT

421 "Overture" and "Underture." Mediterranean tales.
     1972 Harvest 1C-062-29-441, Germany.

     Source: Mozart/The abduction from the Seraglio,
     overture, K. 384, first theme

TUCKER, LOUISE

422 "Graveyard angel." Midnight blue. 1982 Arista
     AL8-8088, US.

     Source: Albinoni/Adagio in G minor for strings and
     organ

423 "Midnight blue." Midnight blue. 1982 Arista AL8-
     8088, US (album); 1982 Arista AS1-9022, US
     (single).

     Source: Beethoven/Sonata no. 8 in C minor, op. 13
     (Pathétique), mvt. 2, first theme

TYMES

424   "Somewhere."   1963 Parkway 891, US (single).

Source: Mozart/Piano sonata no. 1 in C major
Note: This single reached #19 on the Billboard pop
singles chart.

VALENS, RITCHIE

425   "Malagueña."   <u>Ritchie Valens in concert at Pacoima
Jr. High</u>. 1961 Del-Fi DFLP-1214, US.

Source: Albeniz; Lecuona/Malagueña
Note: This instrumental also appears on <u>The best of
Ritchie Valens</u> (1981 Rhino RNDF-200, US).

VANDELLAS. <u>See</u> MARTHA & THE VANDELLAS

VANILLA FUDGE

426   "Eighteenth century: variations on a theme by
Mozart: divertimento no. 13 in F major." <u>The beat
goes on</u>. 1968 Atco SD33-237, US/ 1968 Atlantic
587-100, UK.

Source: Mozart/Divertimento no. 13 in F major

427   "Fur Elise and moonlight sonata." <u>The beat goes on</u>.
1968 Atco SD33-237, US/1968 Atlantic 587-100, UK.

Source: Beethoven/Für Elise; Sonata no. 14 in
C sharp minor, op. 27, no. 2 (Moonlight sonata)

VENTURES

428   "Bach's prelude." <u>Joy--the Ventures play the clas-
sics</u>. 1972 United Artists UAS-5575, US/ 1974
United Artists UAS-29340, UK.

Source: J. S. Bach/Prelude no. ?

429   "Beethoven's sonata in C# minor." <u>Joy--the Ventures
play the classics</u>. 1972 United Artists UAS-5575,
US/1974 United Artists UAS-29340, UK (albums); 1972
United Artists 50903, US (single).

Source: Beethoven/Sonata no. 14 in C sharp minor,
op. 27, no. 2 (Moonlight sonata)

430   "Elise (from Für Elise)." <u>Joy--the Ventures play the
classics</u>. 1972 United Artists UAS-5575, US/ 1974
United Artists UAS-29340, UK.

Source: Beethoven/Für Elise

431   "In a Persian market." Joy--the Ventures play the
       classics. 1972 United Artists UAS-5575, US/ 1974
       United Artists UAS-29340, UK.

       Source: Ketelbey/In a Persian market

432   "Joy (Jesu, joy of man's desiring)." Joy--the
       Ventures play the classics. 1972 United Artists
       UAS-5575, US/ 1974 United Artists UAS-29340, UK
       (albums); 1972 United Artists 50872, US (single).

       Source: J. S. Bach/Jesu, joy of man's desiring (from
       cantata no. 147)
       Note: The single, released Dec. 25, 1971, reached
       #109 on the Billboard pop singles chart.

433   "Melody of joy." Joy--the Ventures play the clas-
       sics. 1972 United Artists UAS-5575, US/ 1974
       United Artists UAS-29340, UK.

       Source: Beethoven/Symphony no. 9 in D minor, op.
       125, mvt. 4, first theme

434   "Mozart forty." Joy--the Ventures play the classics.
       1972 United Artists UAS-5575, US/ 1974 United
       Artists UAS-29340, UK.

       Source: Mozart/Symphony no. 40 in G minor, K. 550

435   "Mozart's minuet." Joy--the Ventures play the
       classics. 1972 United Artists UAS-5575, US/ 1974
       United Artists UAS-29340, UK.

       Source: Mozart/Minuet

436   "One fine day (Un bel di)." Joy--the Ventures play
       the classics. 1972 United Artists UAS-5575, US/
       1974 United Artists UAS-29340, UK.

       Source: Puccini/Madame Butterfly, Un bel di

437   "Peter and the wolf." Joy--the Ventures play the
       classics. 1972 United Artists UAS-5575, US/ 1974
       United Artists UAS-29340, UK (albums); 1972 United
       Artists 50903, US (single).

       Source: Prokofiev/Peter and the wolf, op. 67

438   "Ravel's pavane." Joy--the Ventures play the clas-
       sics. 1972 United Artists UAS-5575, US/ 1974
       United Artists UAS-29340, UK.

       Source: Ravel/Pavane for a dead princess

439   "Swan lake." 1969 Liberty 56153, US (single).

       Source: Tchaikovsky/Swan lake, suite from the
       ballet, op. 20a

VOGUES

440 "A lover's concerto." A lover's concerto. 1971
     Pickwick SPC-3214, US.

     Source: J. S. Bach/Notebook for Anna Magdalena Bach,
     Minuet in G
     Note: This is a version of the song originally
     performed by the Toys (see 419).

WAKEMAN, RICK

441 "Dante period." Lisztomania. 1975 A&M SP-4546, US/
     1975 A&M AMLK-64546, UK.

     Source: Liszt/Dante sonata
     Note: This soundtrack album from the Ken Russell
     film Lisztomania starred Roger Daltrey as Liszt and
     Paul Nicholas as Wagner. The album, arranged by Rick
     Wakeman, reached #145 on the Billboard pop album
     chart. Rick Wakeman has at times been a member of
     the rock group Yes.

442 "Excelsior song." Lisztomania. 1975 A&M SP-4546,
     US/ 1975 A&M AMLK-64546, UK.

     Source: Liszt

443 "The forest." Journey to the centre of the earth.
     1974 A&M SP-3621, US/ 1974 A&M AMLH-63621, UK.

     Source: Grieg/Peer Gynt suite no. 1, op. 46, mvt. 4
     (In the hall of the mountain king)
     Note: The Grieg theme is used only at the conclusion
     of the piece.

444 "Free song." Lisztomania. 1975 A&M SP-4546, US/
     1975 A&M AMLK-64546, UK.

     Source: Liszt/Hungarian rhapsody

445 "Funerailles." Lisztomania. 1975 A&M SP-4546, US/
     1975 A&M AMLK-64546, UK.

     Source: Liszt/Les funerailles

446 "Hell." Lisztomania. 1975 A&M SP-4546, US/ 1975 A&M
     AMLK-64546, UK.

     Source: Liszt

447 "Love's dream." Lisztomania. 1975 A&M SP-4546, US/
     1975 A&M AMLK-64546, UK (albums); 1976 A&M 1779,
     US/ 1976 A&M 7206, UK (Roger Daltrey singles).

     Source: Liszt/Liebestraum no. 3

448 "Master race." <u>Lisztomania</u>. 1975 A&M SP-4546, US/
     1975 A&M AMLK-64546, UK.

     Source: Wagner

449 "Orpheus song." <u>Lisztomania</u>. 1975 A&M SP-4546, US/
     1975 AMLK-64546, UK (albums); 1976 A&M 1779, US/
     1976 A&M 7206, UK (Roger Daltrey singles).

     Source: Liszt/Orpheus: symphonic poem no. 4

450 "Peace at last." <u>Lisztomania</u>. 1975 A&M SP-4546, US/
     1975 A&M AMLK-64546, UK.

     Source: Liszt/Liebestraum no. 3

451 "Rape, pillage & clap." <u>Lisztomania</u>. 1975 A&M
     SP-4546, US/ 1975 A&M AMLK-64546, UK.

     Source: Wagner

452 "Rhapsody in blue." <u>Rhapsodies</u>. 1979 A&M SP-6501,
     US/ 1979 A&M AMLX-68508, UK.

     Source: Gershwin/Rhapsody in blue

453 "Rienzi/Chopsticks fantasia." <u>Lisztomania</u>. 1975 A&M
     SP-4546, US/ 1975 A&M AMLK-64546, UK.

     Source: Wagner/Rienzi; Liszt

454 "Swan lager." <u>Rhapsodies</u>. 1979 A&M SP-6501, US/
     1979 A&M AMLX-68508, UK.

     Source: Tchaikovsky/Swan lake, suite from the
     ballet, op. 20a; Grieg/Piano concerto in A minor, op.
     16

WALSH, JOE

455 "Pavane de la belle au bois dormant." <u>So what</u>. 1974
     ABC Dunhill DSD-50171, US/ 1974 Anchor ABCL-5055,
     UK.

     Source: Ravel/Mother Goose suite, Pavane of the
     sleeping beauty
     Note: This is a synthesizer instrumental.

WEBBER, ANDREW LLOYD. <u>See</u> LLOYD-WEBBER, ANDREW

WILLIE TELL AND THE OVERTURES. <u>See</u> TELL, WILLIE, AND THE
OVERTURES

WILSON, JACKIE

456   "Alone at last." 1960 Brunswick 55170, US/ 1960
      Coral Q-72412, UK (singles).

      Source: Tchaikovsky/Piano concerto no. 1 in B flat
      minor, op. 23
      Note: The single reached #8 on the Billboard pop
      singles chart. It also appears on the album It's all
      a part of love (1971 Brunswick BL-754158, US).

457   "Night." 1960 Brunswick 55166, US (single).

      Source: Saint-Saens/Samson and Delilah, op. 47, act
      2, My heart at thy sweet voice, part B
      Note: This single reached #4 on the Billboard pop
      singles chart. This single, with its lush setting of
      chorus and strings, also appears on the compilations
      Jackie Wilson's greatest hits (1968 Brunswick BL-
      754140, US), It's all a part of love (1971 Brunswick
      BL-754158, US), and The Jackie Wilson story (1983
      Epic EG-38623, US).

WONDER, STEVIE

458   "Ave Maria." Someday at Christmas. 1967 Tamla
      TS-281, US/ 1969 Tamla STML-11085, UK.

      Source: Schubert/Ave Maria (op. 52, no. 6)
      Note: This song, backed up by harp, piano and
      tympani, features a harmonica solo break. It also is
      included on A Motown Christmas (1973 Motown M-795V2,
      1978 Motown 5256ML2, US). Someday at Christmas was
      reissued (1978 Motown 5255ML, US).

WURMAN, HANS

459   "The Italian concerto." Electric nutcracker. 1976
      Ovation OV-1718, US.

      Source: J. S. Bach/Italian concerto, BWV 971

460   "Organ trio sonata, nr. 5 in C major." Electric
      nutcracker. 1976 Ovation OV-1718, US.

      Source: J. S. Bach/Trio sonata no. 5 in C major

461   "Scherzo from The midsummer night's dream." Electric
      nutcracker. 1976 Ovation OV-1718, US.

      Source: Mendelssohn/Midsummer night's dream, scherzo

462   "Suite from the ballet The nutcracker." Electric
      nutcracker. 1976 Ovation OV-1718, US.

      Source: Tchaikovsky/Nutcracker suite, op. 71a

YES

463   "Cans and Brahms." Fragile. 1971 Atlantic SD-7211
       (SD-19132), US/ 1971 Atlantic 2401-019 (K-50009),
       UK.

       Source: Brahms/Symphony no. 4 in E minor, op. 98,
       mvt. 3

464   "Opening." Yessongs. 1973 Atlantic SD3-100, US/
       1973 Atlantic K-60045, UK.

       Source: Stravinsky/Firebird suite
       Note: This is actually a taped orchestra used as an
       introduction to the Yes concert.

ZAPPA, FRANK (and the Mothers of Invention)

465   "Brown shoes don't make it." Absolutely free. 1967
       Verve V6-5013, US/ 1967 Verve SVLP-9174 (2317-035),
       UK.

       Source: Holst/The planets, op. 32
       Note: This also appears on Mothermania: the best of
       the Mothers (1969 Verve V6-5068, US/ 1969 Verve
       SVLP-9239 [2317-047], UK).

466   "The duke of prunes." Absolutely free. 1967 Verve
       V6-5013, US/ 1967 Verve SVLP-9174 (2317-035), UK.

       Source: Stravinsky/The rite of spring; Firebird
       suite
       Note: This also is included on Mothermania: the
       best of the Mothers (1969 Verve V6-5068, US/ 1969
       Verve SVLP-9239 [2317-047], UK) and Frank Zappa's
       Orchestral favorites (1979 DiscReet DSK-2294, US/
       1979 DiscReet K-59212, UK).

467   "Fountain of love." Cruising with Ruben and the
       Jets. 1968 Verve V6-5055, US/ 1968 Verve SVLP-
       9237 (2317-069), UK.

       Source: Stravinsky/The rite of spring
       Note: The opening theme of Stravinsky's piece is one
       of the layers of the fadeout according to Frank
       Zappa, but it is not obvious to the listener.

468   "Invocation and ritual dance of the young pumpkin."
       Absolutely free. 1967 Verve V6-5013, US/ 1967
       Verve SVLP-9174 (2317-035), UK.

       Source: Holst/The planets, op. 32, Jupiter
       Note: This piece, part of "Call any vegetable," also
       appears on Mothermania: the best of the Mothers
       (1969 Verve V6-5068, US/ 1969 Verve SVLP-9239 [2317-
       047], UK).

469 <u>Lumpy gravy</u>. 1967 Verve V6-8741, US/ 1967 Verve
        SVLP-9223 (2317-046), UK.

        Source: Stravinsky/ ? ; Varèse/Ionization; Deserts
        Note: The album's sections, "Lumpy gravy, parts I
        and II," quote from Varèse and Stravinsky. Frank
        Zappa performs with the Abnuceals Emuukha Electric
        Symphony and Chorus, a 50-man session band, including
        many of the members of the Mothers of Invention.

ADDENDA (too late to be added in sequence):

RESIDENTS

469A "Rhapsody in blue." <u>George & James</u>. 1984 Ralph
        RZ-8402, US.

        Source: Gershwin/Rhapsody in blue
        Note: This mostly electronic version of Gershwin's
        piece begins with the famous opening note supplied by
        an air raid siren. The album has one side with
        versions of George Gershwin's classical and Broadway
        music and one side with versions of James Brown's
        soul music. The album is the first volume of a
        projected American Composer Series that will cover
        about twenty composers.

McLAREN, MALCOLM

469B "Madam Butterfly." 1984 Island 096915, US/ 1984
        Virgin/Charisma MALC-512, UK (12" singles).

        Source: Puccini/Madame Butterfly, Un bel di vedremo
        Note: This song integrates lyrics relating to
        Puccini's opera story, the actual aria sung by an
        opera singer, and rock devices known as rapping and
        hip-hop (break dance) rhythms. A 12" picture disc of
        the single was released (1984 Virgin/Charisma MALCS5,
        UK). This single is reported to be one of six
        opera-based songs on McLaren's forthcoming album
        <u>Fans</u>.

QUEEN

469C "It's a hard life." <u>The works</u>. 1984 Capitol ST-
        12322, US/ 1984 EMI EMC-2400141, UK.

        Source: Leoncavallo/I Pagliacci, Vesti la giubba
        Note: The very beginning of the song uses a familiar
        phrase from the Leoncavallo theme.

TOMITA (Isao Tomita)

469D   Canon of the three stars.   1984 RCA ARL1-5184, US.

Source: This album contains Tomita's versions of
pieces by Pachelbel, Rachmaninoff, Albinoni, J. S.
Bach and Villa-Lobos.

469E   Space walk: impressions of an astronaut.   1984 RCA
ARL1-5037, US.

Note: This reissue of numerous Tomita versions of
the classics draws from previous albums and assigns
new titles to the pieces to reflect the space theme.

LAKE, GREG

469F   "I believe in Father Christmas." 1975 Atlantic 3305,
US/ 1975 Manticore K-13511, UK (singles).

Source: Prokofiev/Lieutenant Kije suite, op. 60,
mvt. 4, Troika
Note: This theme follows each verse of the song.
The song also appears on Emerson, Lake & Palmer's
Works, volume 2 (1977 Atlantic SD-19147, US/ 1977
Atlantic K-50422, UK).

SKY

469G   "Troika." Cadmium. 1984 Ariola 205-885, UK.

Source: Prokofiev/Lieutenant Kije suite, op. 60,
mvt. 4, Troika

DEODATO (Eumir Deodato)

469H   "Baubles, bangles and beads." Prelude. 1972 CTI
CTI-6021, US.

Source: Borodin/String quartet no. 2 in D major,
scherzo
Note: The album was reissued as 2001 (CTI CTI-7081,
US).

II.

Classicizin' the Rock

Note: The style and quality of these versions
vary widely, from strict classical style to
pop style orchestral renditions. The name of
the rock group or artist originally performing
the song is given in parentheses after the
title of the song, except in cases where the
entire album is based on one source.

ARANBEE POP SYMPHONY ORCHESTRA

470 Today's pop symphony. 1966 Immediate IMLP-003, UK.

Contents: There's a place (Beatles) -- Rag doll
(Four Seasons) -- I got you babe (Sonny & Cher) -- We
can work it out (Beatles) -- Play with fire (Rolling
Stones) -- Mother's little helper (Rolling Stones) --
In the midnight hour (Wilson Pickett) -- Take it or
leave it (Rolling Stones) -- Sittin' on a fence
(Rolling Stones) -- I don't want to go on without you
(Moody Blues)
Note: This album was produced by Keith Richards of
the Rolling Stones. The credits state that the
orchestra was under his direction and that the album
represents "a new conception of today's hits in
classical style."

ARTHEY, JOHNNY, ORCHESTRA

471 The golden songs of Donovan. 1969 RCA Victor LSP-
4106, US.

Contents: Mellow yellow -- Catch the wind -- There
is a mountain -- Sunny Goodge Street -- Wear your
love like heaven -- Sunshine superman -- Jennifer
Juniper -- Skip along -- Fat angel -- Colours --
Hurdy gurdy man -- Hampstead incident

BAROQUE INEVITABLE

472   The Baroque Inevitable. 1966 Columbia CL-2587
      (mono), CS-9387 (stereo), US.

      Relevant contents: Rainy day women #12 & 35 (Bob
      Dylan) -- Turn-down day (Cyrkle) -- Sunny (Bobby
      Hebb) -- All I really want to do (Bob Dylan; Sonny &
      Cher) -- This door swings both ways (Herman's
      Hermits) -- I couldn't live without your love (Petula
      Clark) -- Wild thing (Troggs) -- Yellow submarine
      (Beatles) -- I can make it with you baby (Pozo-Seco
      Singers) -- Eleanor Rigby (Beatles)
      Note: These are baroque-style instrumental versions
      of rock songs. A note on the album describes it as a
      "baroque-rockque instrumental style popularized by
      Bach, the Beatles, and other notables of the 17th
      through 20th centuries, A.D."

BAXTER, BRUCE

473   Tommy: excerpts from the rock opera. 1973 Pickwick
      SPC-3339, US.

      Contents: You didn't hear it -- Amazing journey --
      Christmas -- The acid queen -- Pinball wizard --
      Smash the mirror -- I'm free -- We're not gonna take
      it
      Note: These excerpts from the Who's Tommy, as
      arranged and conducted by Bruce Baxter, are performed
      by an orchestra, chorus, and soloists.

BEATLES CRACKER SUITE

474   Beatles cracker suite. 1965, UK (EP).

      Contents: It's for you -- Help -- She loves you --
      From me to you -- Ticket to ride -- All my loving
      Note: Origin and performers could not be determined.
      The Beatles' songs are done in classical style.

BEL-AIRE POPS ORCHESTRA

475   Jan and Dean's pop symphony no. 1. 1965 Liberty
      LST-3414 (mono), LST-7414 (stereo), US.

      Note: This album includes orchestral versions of
      songs originally recorded by Jan and Dean.

BOSTON POPS. See FIEDLER, ARTHUR, AND THE BOSTON POPS

BRIARCLIFF STRINGS

476   Briarcliff Strings play Bacharach & David and Simon &
      Garfunkel. 1972 Harmony H-31323, US.

Contents: [relating to Simon & Garfunkel] Sound of silence -- Mrs. Robinson -- Scarborough Fair/Canticle -- Bridge over troubled water

CANDLER, NORMAN, AND HIS MAGIC STRINGS

477   Tribute to John Lennon. 1982 Telefunken AS6-24820, UK.

Contents: Mind games -- Just like starting over -- Woman -- Mother -- Oh my love -- Whatever gets you thru the night -- Tribute to John -- Jealous guy -- Oh Yoko -- Happy Christmas/War is over -- Imagine -- Power to the people
Note: Norman Candler and his Magic Strings perform songs originally recorded by the late John Lennon during his solo career after the Beatles split.

CARAVELLI

478   Caravelli plays Simon and Garfunkel's greatest hits. 1972 Columbia KC-31467, US.

Contents: The sound of silence -- Mrs. Robinson -- Scarborough Fair/Canticle -- The 59th Street Bridge song -- Old friends -- El condor pasa -- Bridge over troubled water -- The boxer -- Cecilia -- Fakin' it -- A hazy shade of winter

CHACKSFIELD, FRANK, AND HIS ORCHESTRA

479   Chacksfield plays Simon and Garfunkel and Jim Webb. 1970 London SP-44151, US.

Relevant contents: Up, up and away (Fifth Dimension) -- Homeward bound (Simon and Garfunkel) -- Mrs. Robinson (Simon and Garfunkel) -- Bridge over troubled water (Simon and Garfunkel) -- Scarborough Fair/Canticle (Simon and Garfunkel) -- Cecilia (Simon and Garfunkel) -- The sound of silence (Simon and Garfunkel) -- MacArthur Park (Richard Harris)
Note: Jim Webb wrote the songs above that were originally recorded by the Fifth Dimension and Richard Harris.

480   Chacksfield plays the Beatles' song book. 1970 London SP-44142, US.

Contents: Get back -- Michelle -- Got to get you into my life -- Yesterday -- Something -- Hey Jude -- A hard day's night -- Norwegian wood -- Ticket to ride -- The fool on the hill -- Come together -- Ob-la-di, ob-la-da

481   The first hits of 1965. 1965 London PS-416, US.

Relevant contents: I feel fine (Beatles) -- She's a
woman (Beatles) -- Downtown (Petula Clark)

FAITH, PERCY, ORCHESTRA (STRINGS)

482   The Beatles album. 1970 Columbia C-30097, US.

Contents: Let it be -- Here, there, and everywhere
-- Norwegian wood -- Michelle -- The ballad of John
and Yoko -- Something -- Eleanor Rigby -- Because --
Lucy in the sky with diamonds -- Yesterday -- The
fool on the hill
Note: This orchestral album of Beatles' songs
reached #179 on the Billboard pop album chart. It
was reissued (19?? Columbia Special Products P-
13279).

483   Jesus Christ superstar. 1971 Columbia C-31042, US.

Note: This album contains orchestra scored selections from Andrew Lloyd-Webber's rock opera Jesus
Christ superstar.

FANTABULOUS STRINGS

484   Sonny and Cher hits. 196? Metro 557, US.

485   Supremes hits. 196? Metro 554, US.

FIEDLER, ARTHUR, AND THE BOSTON POPS

486   Arthur Fiedler and the Boston Pops play the Beatles.
        1969 RCA Red Seal LSC-3117, US.

Relevant contents: Eleanor Rigby -- And I love her
-- Ob-la-di, ob-la-da -- Hey Jude -- With a little
help from my friends -- Yellow submarine -- I want to
hold your hand -- Penny Lane -- The fool on the hill
-- A hard day's night
Note: Curiously, the original 1969 album also
included "Consider yourself" from Oliver and "Those
were the days," both non-Beatles songs. When the
album was reissued (1982 RCA AGL1-4217, US) these
were replaced by the Beatles' "Michelle" and "Yesterday" from Up, up and away (1968 RCA Red Seal LSC-
3041, US). Two singles were released previous to the
album. "I want to hold your hand" (1964 RCA 8378,
US) reached #55 on the Billboard pop singles chart.
"A hard day's night" was released by RCA in 1965. "I
want to hold your hand," "Yesterday," and "Hey Jude"
also appear on the Boston Pops' Greatest hits of the
'60s (1973 RCA Red Seal ARL1-0045, US). "The fool on
the hill" and "Yellow submarine" also appear on their
Greatest hits of the '60s, vol. 2 (1974 RCA Red Seal
ARL1-0509, US).

487   Arthur Fiedler and the Boston Pops play the music of
      Paul Simon. 1971 Polydor PD-5018, US.

      Contents: The sound of silence -- A hazy shade of
      winter -- Scarborough fair/Canticle -- Mrs. Robinson
      -- The dangling conversation -- El condor pasa -- The
      59th Street Bridge song -- Cecilia -- Homeward bound
      -- Old friends -- Bridge over troubled water
      Note: This album of Simon and Garfunkel versions
      reached #196 on the Billboard pop album chart in
      1972.

488   Superstar. 1971 Polydor PD-5008, US.

      Relevant contents: Jesus Christ superstar (Murray
      Head) - What have they done to my song, ma (Melanie)
      -- Proud Mary (Creedence Clearwater Revival) -- Let
      it be (Beatles)

489   Up, up and away. 1968 RCA Red Seal LSC-3041, US.

      Relevant contents: Up, up and away (Fifth Dimension)
      -- Michelle (Beatles) -- A lover's concerto (Toys) --
      Love is blue (Paul Mauriat) -- Yesterday (Beatles)
      Note: "Michelle" and "Yesterday" later reappear on
      the reissue version of Arthur Fiedler and the Boston
      Pops play the Beatles (1982 RCA AGL1-4217, US). "Up,
      up and away" also appears on Boston Pops' Greatest
      hits of the '60s, vol. 2 (1974 RCA Red Seal ARL1-
      0509, US).

GLORIEUX, FRANCOIS

490   Francois Glorieux plays the Beatles. 1978 Vanguard
      79417, US.

      Contents: [composer name in brackets indicates style
      of the piece] Yesterday [Chopin] -- Help/Let it be
      [Schumann] -- Can't buy me love [Gershwin/Prokofiev]
      -- Ob-la-di, ob-la-da [Mozart] -- Hey Jude [Bach] --
      Michelle [Ravel] -- Yellow submarine [Beethoven] --
      Girl/Ob-la-di, ob-la-da [Brahms] -- Norwegian wood
      [Milhaud] -- The fool on the hill [Rachmaninoff] --
      In my life [Debussy] -- Eleanor Rigby [Bartok]
      Note: These piano versions of Beatles' songs are
      performed in the styles of the classical composers as
      noted above.

GOTHAM STRING QUARTET

491   The immortal songs of Bob Dylan. 1965 Philips
      PHM-200-218 (mono), PHS-600-218 (stereo), US.

      Contents: Mr. tambourine man -- When the ship comes
      in -- A hard rain's a-gonna fall -- It ain't me, babe
      -- All I really want to do -- Rainy day women no. 12
      & 35 -- Don't think twice -- One too many mornings --

The times they are a-changin' -- It's all over now,
baby blue -- Like a rolling stone -- Blowin' in the
wind

HEATH, TED, ORCHESTRA

492   The Ted Heath Orchestra plays Beatles, Bach, and
      Bacharach. 1971 London SP-44148, US.

      Relevant contents: [Beatles' songs] Norwegian wood
      -- Hey Jude -- Let it be
      Note: Interspersed with the Beatles' songs are soft
      pop songs written by Burt Bacharach and some themes
      from J. S. Bach.

HOLLYRIDGE STRINGS

493   The Beach Boys song book. 1964 Capitol T-2156
      (mono), ST-2156 (stereo), US.

      Contents: I get around -- Don't worry baby -- She
      knows me too well -- Fun, fun, fun -- Little Saint
      Nick -- In my room -- The warmth of the sun -- Girls
      on the beach -- Shut down -- Surfin' U.S.A. -- Wendy
      Note: This album reached #82 on the Billboard pop
      album chart.

494   The Beach Boys song book, vol. 2. 1967 Capitol
      ST-2749, US.

      Contents: Good vibrations -- God only knows --
      California girls -- Sloop John B -- Caroline, no --
      Surfer girl -- Little deuce coupe -- Help me, Rhonda
      -- Dance, dance, dance -- Be true to your school --
      Wouldn't it be nice

495   The Beatles song book. 1964 Capitol T-2116 (mono),
      ST-2116 (stereo), US.

      Contents: From me to you -- I saw her standing there
      -- Please please me -- P.S. I love you -- Love me do
      -- I want to hold your hand -- Can't buy me love --
      All my loving -- A taste of honey -- Do you want to
      know a secret -- She loves you
      Note: This album reached #15 on the Billboard pop
      album chart. The single "All my loving" (1964
      Capitol 5207, US) reached #93 on the Billboard pop
      singles chart.

496   The Beatles song book, vol. 2. 1965 Capitol T-2202
      (mono), ST-2202 (stereo), US.

      Contents: A hard day's night -- Things we said today
      -- She's a woman -- If I fell -- I'll cry instead --
      I'm happy just to dance with you -- I feel fine -- No
      reply -- I'll be back -- I'm a loser -- I'll follow
      the sun

The Beatles song book, vol. 3. See The new Beatles
   song book

497   The Beatles song book, vol. 4. 1967 Capitol ST-2656,
      US.

      Contents: Strawberry fields forever -- Eleanor Rigby
      -- You've got to hide your love away -- Taxman --
      Good day sunshine -- Act naturally -- Penny Lane --
      Yellow submarine -- Eight days a week -- Drive my car
      -- I've just seen a face

498   The Beatles song book, vol. 5. 1968 Capitol ST-2876,
      US.

      Contents: Magical mystery tour -- I am the walrus --
      The fool on the hill -- A day in the life -- Your
      mother should know -- Baby you're a rich man -- Hello
      goodbye -- She's leaving home -- All you need is love
      -- When I'm sixty-four -- Sgt. Pepper's Lonely Hearts
      Club Band
      Note: Sometimes this album is referred to as The
      Hollyridge Strings play Magical mystery tour.

      The Four Seasons song book. See The Hollyridge
      Strings play instrumental versions of hits by the
      Four Seasons

499   The George, John, Paul and Ringo song book. 1971
      Capitol ST-839, US.

      Contents: Here comes the sun (Beatles) -- Hey Jude
      (Beatles) -- Another day (Paul McCartney) -- Let it
      be (Beatles) -- The long and winding road (Beatles)
      -- My sweet Lord (George Harrison) -- Uncle Albert/
      Admiral Halsey (Paul McCartney) -- Something
      (Beatles) -- It don't come easy (George Harrison) --
      Bangladesh (George Harrison)

500   The Hollyridge Strings play instrumental versions of
      hits made famous by Elvis Presley. 1965 Capitol
      T-2221 (mono), ST-2221 (stereo), US.

      Contents: Love me tender -- Bossa nova baby -- Teddy
      bear -- Heartbreak hotel -- Don't be cruel -- Can't
      help falling in love -- Are you lonesome tonight --
      Return to sender -- Ask me -- Good luck charm -- Kiss
      me quick
      Note: This album reached #144 on the Billboard pop
      album chart.

501   The Hollyridge Strings play instrumental versions of
      hits made famous by the Four Seasons. 1965 Capitol
      T-2199 (mono), ST-2199 (stereo), US.

Contents: Dawn -- Rag doll -- Candy girl -- Ronnie
-- Save it for me -- On Broadway tonight -- Big girls
don't cry -- Walk like a man -- Sherry -- New Mexican
rose -- Stay
Note: This album sometimes is referred to as The
Four Seasons song book.

The Hollyridge Strings play Magical mystery tour.
   See The Beatles song book, vol. 5

502   The Hollyridge Strings play the hits of Simon and
      Garfunkel. 1968 Capitol ST-2998, US.

503   The new Beatles song book. 1966 Capitol T-2429
      (mono), ST-2429 (stereo), US.

      Contents: The night before -- Yesterday -- Ticket to
      ride -- Norwegian wood -- Michelle -- Help! -- Day
      tripper -- Nowhere man -- And I love her -- Girl --
      We can work it out
      Note: This album is sometimes referred to as The
      Beatles song book, vol. 3.

KING'S SINGERS

504   Keep on changing. 1975 EMI EMC-3076, US.

      Relevant contents: Life on Mars? (David Bowie) -- A
      horse with no name (America)
      Note: The King's Singers, a male vocal sextet well
      known for their madrigals and motets, also perform
      rock songs with a classical tinge.

505   The King's Singers. 1972 One-Up OU-2118, UK.

      Relevant contents: She's leaving home (Beatles) --
      The windmills of your mind (Dusty Springfield) --
      Morning has broken (Cat Stevens) -- My colouring book
      (Kitty Kallen; Sandy Stewart)
      Note: "The windmills of your mind" also appears on
      the compilation By request (1983 Moss Music Group
      MMG-1141, US).

506   Lollipops. c1974, 1975 EMI EMC-3093, US.

      Relevant contents: I'm a train (Albert Hammond) --
      Ding a dong/Killing me softly with his song (Teach-
      ins/Roberta Flack) -- After the gold rush (Neil
      Young; Prelude) -- Ob-la-di, ob-la-da (Beatles)
      Note: "I'm a train," "After the gold rush," and
      "Ob-la-di, ob-la-da" also appear in live versions on
      10th anniversary concert: record 2 (1978 EMI KS-
      1002, Moss Music Group MMG-1102, US).

507 <u>New day</u>. 1980 Moss Music Group MMG-1116, US.

Relevant contents: Three times a lady (Commodores) -- Can't buy me love (Beatles) -- Here comes the sun (Beatles) -- Money, money, money (Abba) -- Could it be magic (Barry Manilow)
Note: "Three times a lady" and "Can't buy me love" also appaer on the compilation <u>By request</u> (1983 Moss Music Group MMG-1141, US).

508 <u>Out of the blue</u>. 1974 EMI EMC-3023, Moss Music Group MMG-1109, US.

Relevant contents: The fool on the hill (Beatles)

509 <u>Tempus fugit</u>. 1978 EMI EMC-3268, Moss Music Group MMG-1112, US.

Relevant contents: Monday Monday (Mamas & the Papas) -- Everything I own (Bread) -- 59th Street Bridge song: feelin' groovy (Simon and Garfunkel; Harpers Bizarre) -- Going nowhere (Los Bravos) -- Space oddity (David Bowie) -- Honky cat (Elton John) -- Mr. tambourine man (Bob Dylan; Byrds) -- Don't let the sun go down on me (Elton John) -- God only knows (Beach Boys) -- Things we said today (Beatles) -- Disney girls: 1957 (Beach Boys) -- Strawberry fields forever (Beatles)
Note: A strawberry scratch n' sniff decorated single was released for "Strawberry fields forever" (1978 EMI).

KNIGHT, PETER, AND HIS ORCHESTRA

510 <u>Instrumental Beatles themes from Sgt. Pepper's Lonely Hearts Club Band</u>. 1967 Mercury SR-61132, US.

KOSTELANETZ, ANDRE

511 <u>Andre Kostelanetz plays Chicago</u>. 1971 Columbia C-31002, US.

Contents: Wake up sunshine -- Fancy colours -- Make me smile -- Does anybody really know what time it is? -- Questions 67 and 68 -- Colour my world -- Beginnings -- 25 or 6 to 4 -- Where do we go from here? -- It better end soon -- Flight 602
Note: These are orchestral arrangements of songs originally performed by the rock group Chicago.

LEWIS, VIC, AND HIS ORCHESTRA

512 <u>Donovan my way</u>. 1968 Epic BN-26418, US.

Contents: Sunshine superman -- There is a mountain -- Poor cow -- Lelainia [Lalena] -- Lord of the reedy

river -- Mellow yellow -- Hurdy gurdy man -- Catch
the wind -- Young girl blues -- A sunny day -- Three
king fishers -- Jennifer Juniper
Note: These versions of Donovan's songs feature
strings, winds, harpsichord, bass and percussion.

LIVERPOOL STRINGS

513   Herman's Hermits greatest hits. 196? Metro MS-560.

Note: These are orchestral versions of songs
originally performed by the '60s rock group Herman's
Hermits.

LIVING STRINGS

514   Alice's restaurant. 1967 RCA Camden 2395, US. (Arlo
        Guthrie)

515   Beatles songs. 1970 RCA Camden CAS-2438, US.

516   I'm a believer and other Monkees' hits. 1967 RCA
        Camden CAL-2148, US.

517   Music from the rock opera Jesus Christ superstar.
        1971 RCA Camden CAS-2481, US. (Andrew Lloyd-
        Webber)

518   Songs of the swingin' sixties. 1967 RCA Camden 2397,
        US.

LONDON CONCERT ORCHESTRA

519   The London Concert Orchestra plays Elton John. 19??
        Nova NSK-192, UK (cassette).

Contents: Goodbye yellow brick road -- Lucy in the
sky with diamonds -- Bennie and the Jets -- Rocket
man -- Elton's journey -- Honky cat -- Island girl --
Philadelphia freedom -- Don't let the sun go down on
me -- John strings

520   The London Concert Orchestra plays Elvis. 19?? Nova
        NSK-143, UK (cassette).

Contents: Hound dog -- Are you lonesome tonight? --
Heartbreak hotel -- I want you, I need you, I love
you -- Jailhouse rock -- Love me tender -- Fools rush
in -- Lonesome railroad blues -- How great Thou art
-- Hawaiian bells

521   The London Concert Orchestra plays the Beach Boys.
        19?? Nova NSK-161, UK (cassette).

Contents: California girls -- Help me, Rhonda -- I
get around -- Goodtime feelin' -- Good vibrations --

Fun, fun, fun -- Don't worry baby -- Goodbye baby --
Wouldn't it be nice -- Darlin'

522   The London Concert Orchestra plays the Beatles.   19??
        Nova NSK-129, UK (cassette).

Contents: Hey Jude -- Yesterday -- Eleanor Rigby --
She loves you -- Lucy in the sky with diamonds -- A
hard day's night -- I want to hold your hand -- All
you need is love -- Penny Lane -- Michelle

LONDON FESTIVAL ORCHESTRA

523   Close to you.   1971 London SP-44156, US.

Relevant contents: Something (Beatles) -- Don't play
that song (Ben E. King; Aretha Franklin) -- The long
and winding road (Beatles) -- Make it with you
(Bread) -- Cecilia (Simon and Garfunkel) -- My baby
loves lovin' (White Plains) -- The sound of silence
(Simon and Garfunkel)

524   Destination love.   1969 London SP-44135, US.

Relevant contents: My cherie amour (Stevie Wonder)
-- Aquarius (Fifth Dimension) -- Classical gas (Mason
Williams) -- Baby, I love you (Ronettes; Andy Kim) --
Good morning starshine (Oliver)

525   Here come the hits.   1970 London SP-44143, US.

Relevant contents: Arizona (Mark Lindsay) -- Bridge
over troubled water (Simon and Garfunkel) -- Sugar
sugar (Archies) -- Daydream (Lovin' Spoonful)

LONDON PHILHARMONIC ORCHESTRA

526   Classic case of funk.   1983 Warwick WW-5130, UK.

LONDON SYMPHONY ORCHESTRA

527   Best of classic rock.   1982 K-tel ONE-1080, UK.

Contents: Medley -- Eye of the tiger (Survivor) --
Whole lotta love (Led Zeppelin) -- Baker Street
(Gerry Rafferty) -- Paint it black (Rolling Stones)
-- Get back (Beatles) -- Rhapsody in black -- Reach
out I'll be there (Four Tops) -- Standing in the
shadows of love (Four Tops) -- Ruby Tuesday (Rolling
Stones) -- Bohemian rhapsody (Queen) -- First time
ever I saw your face (Roberta Flack) -- Sailing
(Christopher Cross)

528   Classic rock, volume one.   1979 RSO RS-1-3043, US/
        1977 K-tel ?, UK.

Contents: Bohemian rhapsody (Queen) -- Nights in
white satin (Moody Blues) -- Whole lotta love (Led
Zeppelin) -- Paint it black (Rolling Stones) -- A
whiter shade of pale (Procol Harum) -- Lucy in the
sky with diamonds (Beatles) -- Without you (Nilsson)
-- I'm not in love (10CC)
Note: The Royal Choral Society also appears on this
album.

529   Hooked on rock classics. 1982 RCA AFL1-4608, US.

Contents: Rock classics medley -- Eye of the tiger
(Survivor) -- Baker Street (Gerry Rafferty) -- Layla
(Derek and the Dominos) -- Get back (Beatles) --
Fanfare/Intro. -- Rhapsody in black -- Reach out I'll
be there (Four Tops) -- Standing in the shadows of
love (Four Tops) -- The first time ever I saw your
face (Roberta Flack) -- Ruby Tuesday (Rolling Stones)
-- Paint it black (Rolling Stones)
Note: The Royal Choral Society also appears on this
album.

530   Rhapsody in black. 1979 K-tel ONE-1063, UK.

Contents: Fanfare/Intro. -- Rhapsody in black --
Reach out I'll be there (Four Tops) -- The first time
ever I saw your face (Roberta Flack) -- Superstition
(Stevie Wonder) -- Standing in the shadows of love
(Four Tops) -- Don't leave me this way (Thelma
Houston) -- Tears of a clown (Miracles) -- Rasputin
(Boney M) -- I heard it through the grapevine (Marvin
Gaye; Gladys Knight and the Pips) -- Ain't no moun-
tain high enough (Marvin Gaye/Tammi Terrell; Diana
Ross)
Note: The Royal Choral Society also appears on this
album.

531   The second movement. 1978 RSO RS-1-3073, US/ 1978
      K-tel NE-1039, UK.

Contents: Pinball wizard (Who) -- Hey Joe (Leaves;
Jimi Hendrix) -- A day in the life (Beatles) --
Question (Moody Blues) -- Space oddity (David Bowie)
-- God only knows (Beach Boys) -- River deep, moun-
tain high (Ike and Tina Turner) -- American trilogy
(Mickey Newbury)
Note: This is actually volume two of Classic Rock.
The Royal Choral Society also appears on The Second
Movement.

532   Zappa, volume 1. 1983 Barking Pumpkin FW-38820, US.

Contents: Sad Jane -- Pedro's dowry -- Envelopes --
Mo 'n Herb's vacation (1st movement, 2nd movement,
3rd movement)
Note: This music was composed and arranged by Frank

Zappa for large orchestra. Some of the pieces originally appeared on Zappa's earlier rock albums using a small rock ensemble. "Pedro's dowry" appeared on <u>Orchestral favorites</u> and "Envelopes" appeared on <u>Ship arriving too late to save a drowning witch</u>. After presenting these four works in a live concert by the London Symphony Orchestra, they were recorded in a studio for release.

533   <u>Zappa, volume 2</u>. due ?

MANHATTAN STRINGS

534   <u>The Manhattan Strings play instrumental versions of hits made famous by the Monkees</u>. 1967 Tower ST-5067, US.

MARTIN, GEORGE, ORCHESTRA

535   <u>The Beatle girls</u>. 1966 United Artists UAL-3539 (mono), UAS-6539 (stereo), US/ 1967 United Artists SULP-1157, UK.

Contents: Girl -- Eleanor Rigby -- She said she said -- I'm only sleeping -- Anna (Go to him) -- Michelle -- Got to get you into my life -- Woman -- Yellow submarine -- Here, there and everywhere -- And your bird can sing -- Good day sunshine
Note: George Martin was the Beatles' producer. He issued several instrumental albums of Beatles' songs recorded by his orchestra.

536   <u>By George!</u> 1970 Sunset SLS-50182, UK.

Relevant contents: Sgt. Pepper's Lonely Hearts Club Band -- I am the walrus
Note: This album may be the same as <u>London by George</u> (1968 United Artists UAS-6647, US).

537   <u>George Martin scores instrumental versions of the hits</u>. 1965 United Artists UAS-6420, US.

Relevant contents: I feel fine -- P.S. I love you -- No reply
Note: A single was released for "I feel fine" (1965 Parlophone R-5256, UK).

538   <u>A hard day's night</u>. 1964 United Artists UAS-6383, US.

Contents: I'll cry instead -- Ringo's theme (This boy) -- If I fell -- I'm happy just to dance with you -- A hard day's night -- I should have known better -- I want to hold your hand -- Can't buy me love -- She loves you -- And I love her -- All my loving -- Don't bother me -- Tell me why

Note: This is an instrumental album. On the U.S.
soundtrack album of the Beatles' film A hard day's
night (1964 United Artists UAL-3366 [mono], UAS-6366
[stereo], US; Capitol SW-11921, US), the George
Martin Orchestra plays instrumental versions of the
Beatles' songs "I should have known better," "And I
love her," "Ringo's theme (This boy)," and "A hard
day's night." In the U.K., there was also a four-
song EP entitled Music from the film "A hard day's
night" (1965 Parlophone GEP-8930, UK) including "And
I love her," "Ringo's theme (This boy)," "A hard
day's night," and "If I fell." Singles released by
the George Martin Orchestra were "A hard day's
night/I should have known better" (1964 United
Artists 750, US) and "Ringo's theme (This boy)/And I
love her" (1964 United Artists 745, US/ 1964 Parlophone R-5166, UK). "Ringo's theme" reached #53 on
the Billboard pop singles chart.

539 Help! and other instrumental versions of the Beatles
        songs. 1965 United Artists UAS-6448, US/ 1965
        Columbia TWO-102, UK.

        Contents: Help! -- Another girl -- You're gonna lose
        that girl -- I need you -- You've got to hide your
        love away -- The night before -- Ticket to ride --
        Auntie Gin's theme (I've just seen a face) -- That's
        a nice hat CAP (It's only love) -- Tell me what you
        see -- Scrambled egg (Yesterday)
        Note: This is an all instrumental album. A single
        of "Yesterday/Another girl" was released (1965 Parlo-
        phone R-5375, UK). In addition, the George Martin
        Orchestra recorded a portion of the U.S. soundtrack
        album of the Beatles' film Help! (1965 Capitol
        SMAS-2386, US) including Beatles-based "From me to
        you fantasy," "Another hard day's night" and "You
        can't do that."

        London by George. See By George!

540 Off the Beatle track: versions of the Beatles big
        hits. 1964 United Artists UAL-3377 (mono), UAS-
        6377 (stereo), US/ 1964 Parlophone PCS-3057, UK.

        Contents: All my loving -- Don't bother me -- Can't
        buy me love -- All I've got to do -- I saw her
        standing there -- She loves you -- From me to you --
        There's a place -- This boy -- Please please me --
        Little child -- I want to hold your hand
        Note: This album was reissued in the U.K. (198? See
        for Miles/Charly CM-101, UK). In the U.K., the
        single "All my loving/I saw her standing there" was
        released (1964 Parlophone R-5135, UK).

541 Yellow submarine. 1969 Apple SW-153, US/ 1969 Apple
        PMC(PCS)-7070, UK.

Note: This Beatles' film soundtrack album includes a piece by the George Martin Orchestra, using a Lennon-McCartney composed tune, entitled "Yellow submarine in Pepper Land."

MAURIAT, PAUL, AND HIS ORCHESTRA

542 Blooming hits. 1968 Philips PHS-600-248, US.

Relevant contents: Penny Lane (Beatles) -- This is my song (Petula Clark) -- There's a kind of hush (Herman's Hermits) -- Puppet on a string (Elvis Presley) -- Mama (B. J. Thomas)

543 Doing my thing. 1969 Philips PHS-600-292, US.

Relevant contents: Hey Jude (Beatles) -- Elenore (Turtles) -- Abraham, Martin & John (Dion)

METROPOLITAN POPS ORCHESTRA

544 Bob Dylan hits. 196? Metro 597, US.

545 Peter, Paul and Mary hits. 196? Metro 596, US.

MONTENEGRO, HUGO

546 Hugo in Wonder-land. 1974 RCA APL1-0413, US.

Contents: Living for the city -- Too high -- Superstition -- You are the sunshine of my life -- My cherie amour -- Higher ground -- Don't you worry 'bout a thing -- Shoo-bee-doo-bee-doo-do-day -- You've got it bad girl -- All in love is fair
Note: These instrumentals were originally recorded by Stevie Wonder as songs.

547 Rocket man: a tribute to Elton John. 1975 RCA APL1-1024, US.

Contents: Blastoff -- Rocket man -- The bitch is back -- Goodbye yellow brick road -- Philadelphia freedom -- Take me to the pilot -- Your song -- Lowdown hoedown -- Daniel -- Lucy in the sky with diamonds -- Splashdown
Note: These are instrumental versions of songs once recorded by Elton John.

NEW RENAISSANCE SOCIETY

548 Baroque n' Stones. 1966 Hanna-Barbera HLP-8504 (mono), HLP-9504 (stereo), US.

Contents: Under the boardwalk medley -- Nineteenth nervous breakdown -- Get off of my cloud -- As tears go by -- Satisfaction -- Play with fire -- Tell me -- Cry to me

Note: These pieces are baroque-style renditions of
songs originally performed by the Rolling Stones.

NITZSCHE, JACK, AND ORCHESTRA

549 <u>Dance to the hits of the Beatles</u>. 1965 Reprise 6115,
US.

Note: Orchestral versions of Beatles' songs are
performed on this album in a pop style.

OLDHAM, ANDREW, ORCHESTRA

550 <u>The Rolling Stones songbook</u>. 1966 London PS-457, US/
1966 Decca LK-4796, UK.

Contents: Blue turns to grey -- Satisfaction -- You
better move on -- Time is on my side -- Heart of
stone -- As tears go by -- Play with fire -- Theme
for a Rolling Stone -- Tell me -- Congratulations --
The last time
Note: Andrew Loog Oldham was at one time a producer
for the Rolling Stones.

551 <u>16 hip hits</u>. 1964 Decca/Ace of Clubs ACL-1180, UK.

Relevant contents: Needles and pins (Searchers) --
Blowin' in the wind (Bob Dylan) -- I just don't know
what to do with myself (Dusty Springfield) -- La
bamba (Tokens) -- Then he kissed me (Crystals) -- Do
wah diddy diddy (Manfred Mann) -- I want to hold your
hand (Beatles) -- My boy Lollipop (Millie Small) --
Da doo ron ron (Crystals) -- Memphis (Lonnie Mack;
Johnny Rivers) -- You're no good (Betty Everett;
Swinging Blue Jeans) -- I wanna be your man (Beatles)
-- Chapel of love (Dixie Cups)
Note: The other three pieces are Oldham's own
compositions and not versions of rock songs.

101 STRINGS

552 <u>Famous hits of Simon and Garfunkel</u>. 197? Alshire
S-5156, US.

Contents: The sound of silence -- I am a rock --
Trav'lin' again -- Feelin' groovy -- Scarborough fair
-- Homeward bound -- Orange Grove Avenue -- Mrs.
Robinson -- When the trees that are green turn to
brown -- The boxer
Note: This album also has been known as <u>Million
seller hits written by Simon and Garfunkel</u>, <u>Hits of
Simon and Garfunkel</u>, and <u>Million seller hits of today
written by Simon and Garfunkel</u>. A single was re-
leased of "The sound of silence" (197? Alshire 4510,
US).

553 Hits from the rock opera "Jesus Christ superstar."
     1972 Alshire S-5252, US.

     Contents: I don't know how to love him -- Superstar
     -- John nineteen forty-one -- Everything's alright --
     + others

     Hits made famous by the Beatles. See 101 Strings
     play hits written by the Beatles

554 Hits made famous by the Supremes. 197? Alshire
     S-5105, US.

     Contents: Stop! in the name of love -- It's so
     exciting -- You can't hurry love -- Baby love -- My
     world is empty without you -- I hear a symphony --
     Where did our love go? -- Baby, let's smooth it over
     -- Back in my arms again -- In and out of love
     Note: An alternate title is Million seller hits of
     the Supremes.

     Hits of Simon and Garfunkel. See Famous hits of
     Simon and Garfunkel

     Hits written by Carole King. See A portrait of
     Carole

     Million seller hits of the Supremes. See Hits made
     famous by the Supremes

     Million seller hits of today written by Simon and
     Garfunkel. See Famous hits of Simon and Garfunkel

     Million seller hits written by Simon and Garfunkel.
     See Famous hits of Simon and Garfunkel

     Million seller hits written by the Beatles. See 101
     Strings play hits written by the Beatles

     101 Strings Orchestra performs hit songs by Carole
     King. See A portrait of Carole

555 101 Strings play a tribute to Elvis Presley. 197?
     Alshire 5348, US.

     Contents: Heartbreak hotel -- Lonesome railroad
     blues -- How great Thou art -- Hawaiian bells --
     Jailhouse rock -- I want you, I need you, I love you
     -- Fools rush in -- Love me tender -- Are you lone-
     some tonight? -- Hound dog

556 101 Strings play hits made famous by Stevie Wonder
     and Gladys Knight. 1974 Alshire S-5314, US.

557 101 Strings play hits made famous by the Beach Boys.
     197? Alshire 5342, US.

Contents: California girls -- Help me, Rhonda -- I
get around -- Goodtime feelin' -- Good vibrations --
Fun, fun, fun -- Don't worry baby -- Goodbye baby --
Wouldn't it be nice -- Darlin'

558   101 Strings play hits written by the Beatles.   196?
      Alshire S-5111, US.

Contents: A hard day's night -- Penny Lane --
Yesterday -- Six pence and you -- She loves you --
All you need is love -- I want to hold your hand --
Blues for the guru -- Eleanor Ribgy -- Tropic of
Chelsea
Note: This album has also been titled Million seller
hits written by the Beatles, 101 Strings play the
hits of the Beatles and Hits made famous by the
Beatles. A 1977 reissue substitutes "Hey Jude" for
"Penny Lane" and "House of the rising sun" for "She
loves you."

101 Strings play songs written by Carole King. See A
   portrait of Carole

101 Strings play the hits of the Beatles. See 101
   Strings play hits written by the Beatles

559   A portrait of Carole. 1972 Alshire S-5278, US.

Contents: Hey girl -- Up on the roof -- Tapestry --
Portrait of Carole -- It's too late -- It's going to
take some time -- Chains -- Just once in my life --
Go away little girl -- King for a day
Note: Alternate album titles are Hits written by
Carole King, 101 Strings Orchestra performs hit songs
by Carole King, and 101 Strings play songs written by
Carole King.

560   Songs made famous by Elton John. 1976 Alshire
      S-5239, US.

Contents: Goodbye yellow brick road -- Lucy in the
sky with diamonds -- Bennie and the Jets -- Rocket
man -- Elton's journey -- Honky cat -- Island girl --
Philadelphia freedom -- Don't let the sun go down on
me -- John strings

561   Soul hits. 197? Alshire S-5237, US.

562   A tribute to John Lennon. 198? Alshire ?, US.

Contents (Beatles): Hey Jude -- Yesterday -- Eleanor
Rigby -- She loves you -- Lucy in the sky with
diamonds -- A hard day's night -- I want to hold your
hand -- All you need is love -- Penny Lane --
Michelle

PAGE, LARRY, ORCHESTRA

563 Kinky music. 1965 Decca ?, UK.

Contents: Tired of waiting for you -- All day and
all of the night -- Revenge -- You really got me --
+ others
Note: This album includes songs, originally performed by the Kinks, arranged by Ray Davies for
orchestra. Larry Page was the original producer of
the Kinks. The album was reissued (1983 Rhino
RNLP-058, US).

PARIS OPERA ORCHESTRA

564 The baroque connection. 1973 Angel S-37000, US.

Note: This album presents "great film music in the
style of Handel and Vivaldi" and includes a version
of the Beatles' "Let it be" from the film of the same
title.

POP-ROCK SYMPHONIA

565 Orchestral pops collection. 1983 Cambra CR-093, UK.

Partial contents: Take it away (Paul McCartney) --
Come on Eileen (Dexy's Midnight Runners) -- Super
trouper (Abba)

PORTSMOUTH SINFONIA

566 20 classic rock classics. 1979 Phonogram.

Partial contents: Pinball wizard (Who) -- A whiter
shade of pale (Procol Harum) -- God only knows (Beach
Boys)

POURCEL, FRANCK, AND HIS ORCHESTRA

567 Digital around the world. 1982 EMI Imports.

Partial contents: Bette Davis eyes (Kim Carnes) --
Logical song (Supertramp)

568 Frank Pourcel meets the Beatles. 1972 Columbia
     TWO-371, UK.

Contents: Let it be -- I, me, mine -- Penny Lane --
Michelle -- Here, there, and everywhere -- The long
and winding road -- Eleanor Rigby -- Hey Jude --
Ob-la-di, Ob-la-da -- Don't let me down -- Girl --
Yesterday -- Goodbye
Note: Beatles' songs are done with baroque and
romantic flourishes on this album.

POWELL, ANDREW, AND PHILHARMONIA ORCHESTRA

569   Andrew Powell and Philharmonia Orchestra play the
      best of the Alan Parsons Project. 1983 EMI EMTV-
      1077391, UK.

      Contents: Lucifer/Mammagamma -- Time -- Games people
      play -- I robot suite -- Damned if I do -- Pavane --
      What goes up -- Eye in the sky -- Old and wise
      Note: Andrew Powell arranges and conducts the string
      sections of Alan Parsons Project albums.

REGAL FUNKHARMONIC ORCHESTRA

570   Strung out on Motown. 1982 Motown 6014, US.

      Contents: Strung out on Motown medley -- Strung out
      on the Supremes medley -- Strung out on the Tempta-
      tions medley -- Strung out on the Four Tops medley --
      Strung out on the Commodores medley -- Strung out on
      Rick James medley
      Note: The single released from this album was
      "Strung out on Motown medley/Strung out on the
      Commodores medley" (1982 Motown 1629, US).

RIFKIN, JOSHUA

571   The baroque Beatles book. 1965 Elektra EKS-7306, US.

      Contents: The royal Beatleworks musicke, MBE 1963:
      1) Overture - I want to hold your hand, 2) Rejouis-
      sance - I'll cry instead, 3) La paix - Things we said
      today, 4) L'amour s'en cachant - You've got to hide
      your love away/Ticket to ride -- Epstein variations,
      MBE 69A: Hold me tight (Murray the Klavierkitzler)
      -- "Last night I said," cantata for the third Satur-
      day after Shea Stadium, MBE 58,000: 1) Chorus:
      "Last night I said" - Please please me, 2) Recita-
      tive: "In they came joking," Aria: "When I was
      younger" - Help, 3) Chorale: "You know, if you break
      my heart" - I'll be back -- Trio sonata: Das käfer-
      lein, MBE 0041/4: 4) Grave; allegro; grave - Eight
      days a week, 5) Quodlibette - She loves you; Thank
      you girl; Hard day's night
      Note: Joshua Rifkin arranged Beatles' tunes in
      baroque style for his Baroque Ensemble of the Mersey-
      side Kammermusik-Gesellschaft. The single released
      was "You've got to hide your love away/Ticket to
      ride" (1965 Elektra 45602, US).

ROCKIN' STRINGS

572   The Rockin' Strings. 1960 Decca DL7-8998, US.

ROMANTIQUE ORCHESTRA

573   Memories -- beautiful love songs collection. 1983
      Cambra CR-092, UK.

Partial contents: Ebony and ivory (Paul McCartney)
-- Your song (Elton John) -- Nights in white satin
(Moody Blues) -- She's gone (Hall and Oates) -- 50
ways to leave your lover (Paul Simon) -- If you leave
me now (Chicago)

ROYAL LIVERPOOL PHILHARMONIC ORCHESTRA

574   The Beatles concerto. 1979 MMG MMG-1121, US.

Contents: The Beatles concerto: 1) Maestoso-allegro
moderato: She loves you, Eleanor Rigby, Yesterday,
All my loving, Hey Jude; 2) Andante espressivo:
Here, there and everywhere; Something; 3) Presto:
Can't buy me love, The long and winding road -- Six
Beatles impressions: 1) The fool on the hill, 2)
Lucy in the sky with dimaonds, 3) Michelle, 4)
Maxwell's silver hammer, 5) Here comes the sun, 6) A
hard day's night
Note: The Beatles' tunes were arranged by John
Rutter for orchestra and duo pianists (Peter Rostal
and Paul Schaefer).

ROYAL PHILHARMONIC ORCHESTRA

575   Arrested -- music of Police. 1983 RCA RCALP-8001,
      UK.

Contents: Overture -- De do do do de da da da --
Released -- Every little thing she does is magic --
Roxanne -- Truth hits everybody -- Arrested -- Don't
stand so close to me -- Message in a bottle --
Invisible sun -- Walking on the moon -- Finale

576   Heavy metal: the score. 1981 Full Moon/Asylum
      5E-547, US.

Note: This is the orchestral score from the 1981
film Heavy metal, as opposed to the album of rock
songs excerpted from the film.

577   Love classics. 1983 Nouveau NML-1003, UK.

Relevant contents: Three times a lady (Commodores)
-- If you leave me now (Chicago) -- Miss you nights
(Cliff Richard) -- Imagine (John Lennon)

578   The Royal Philharmonic Orchestra plays the Beatles.
      1983 Solid Rock Foundation SRFL-1001, UK.

579   The Royal Philharmonic Orchestra plays the Queen
      collection. 1982 EMI Angel S-37910, US.

Contents: Queen medley -- Flash -- Play the game --
We are the champions -- Don't stop me now -- Love of
my life -- Killer queen -- You're my best friend --
Teo torriate -- Crazy little thing called love --
Bohemian rhapsody -- Under pressure

Note: Louis Clark conducts the Royal Philharmonic
Orchestra and the Royal Choral Society. The single
released was "Bohemian rhapsody/Queen medley" (1982
Angel 5128, US).

SCARBOROUGH STRINGS AND HARPSICHORD

580   A whiter shade of pale. 19?? Superscope 2-A022 (8
track), 1-A022 (cassette), US.

Note: A version of Procol Harum's "A whiter shade of
pale" probably appears on this recording. This is a
double twist since Procol Harum's song is Bach-based
rock, here done in baroque style by strings.

SPIEGEL, FRITZ

581   Eine kleine Beatlemusik. 1964 HMV 7EG-8887, UK (EP).

Contents: She loves you -- I'll get you -- I want to
hold your hand -- A hard day's night -- Please please
me -- All my loving
Note: Fritz Spiegel devised these classically styled
versions of Beatles' tunes and Harry Wild arranged
them.

THRILLINGTON, PERCY "THRILLS"

582   Thrillington. 1977 Capitol ST-11642, US/ 1977 EMI
EMC-3175, UK.

Contents: Too many people -- 3 legs -- Ram on --
Dear boy -- Uncle Albert/Admiral Halsey -- Smile away
-- Heart of the country -- Monkberry moon delight --
Eat at home -- Long haired lady -- Back seat of my
car
Note: Supposedly, Paul McCartney was actually behind
this album. The instrumental pieces are versions of
songs from his 1971 album Ram. The single released
from Thrillington in the U.K. was "Eat at home/Uncle
Albert" (1977 EMI, UK).

VARIOUS ORCHESTRAS

583   Indian reservation and other top pop hits. 1971 RCA
Camden CAS-2531, US.

Contents: The lament of the Cherokee Indian reserva-
tion (The Raiders) -- Wild horses (Rolling Stones) --
Joy to the world (Three Dog Night) -- Brown sugar
(Rolling Stones) -- I'm a believer (Monkees) --
Bridge over troubled water (Simon and Garfunkel) -- I
don't know how to love him (Yvonne Elliman) -- The
sound of silence (Simon and Garfunkel) -- Superstar
(Murray Head)
Note: Various orchestras and instrumental ensembles
appear on this album.

WILLIAMS, JOHN

584   A portrait of John Williams.   1982 CBS Masterworks
         M-37791, US.

      Note: This album includes an orchestrated version of
      the Beatles' "Fool on the hill" by guitarist John
      Williams.

ADDENDA (too late to be added in sequence):

BERLIN PHILHARMONIC CELLISTS

584A   Beatles in classic.   1984 Teldec AS6-25579, UK.

      Contents: Yellow submarine -- Let it be -- Something
      -- Fool on the hill -- Yesterday -- Michelle -- Hard
      day's night -- Norwegian wood -- Can't buy me love --
      Hey Jude -- Here, there and everywhere

BOULEZ, PIERRE

584B   Boulez conducts Zappa: the perfect stranger and
         other chamber works.   1984 EMI Angel DS-38170, US.

      Note: Frank Zappa composed these works for small
      orchestra, one work being commissioned by conductor
      Pierre Boulez. The pieces were recorded by the
      Ensemble InterContemporain and the Barking Pumpkin
      Digital Gratification Consort.

III.
Other Connections Between Rock and the Classics

A. Rock Groups or Artists Recording with
    Established Orchestras and Choruses

ALL THIS AND WORLD WAR II

585 All this and World War II. 1976 20th Century 2T-522,
     US/ 1976 Riva RVLP-2, UK.

     Contents: Magical mystery tour (Ambrosia) -- Lucy in
     the sky with diamonds (Elton John) -- Golden
     slumbers/Carry that weight (Bee Gees) -- I am the
     walrus (Leo Sayer) -- She's leaving home (Bryan
     Ferry) -- Lovely Rita (Roy Wood) -- When I'm sixty-
     four (Keith Moon) -- Get back (Rod Stewart) -- Let it
     be (Leo Sayer) -- Yesterday (David Essex) -- With a
     little help from my friends/Nowhere man (Jeff Lynne)
     -- Because (Lynsey DePaul) -- She came in through the
     bathroom window (Bee Gees) -- Michelle (Richard
     Cocciante) -- We can work it out (Four Seasons) --
     The fool on the hill (Helen Reddy) -- Maxwell's
     silver hammer (Frankie Laine) -- Hey Jude (Brothers
     Johnson) -- Polythene Pam (Roy Wood) -- Sun king (Bee
     Gees) -- Getting better (Status Quo) -- The long and
     winding road (Leo Sayer) -- Help (Henry Gross) --
     Strawberry fields forever (Peter Gabriel) -- A day in
     the life (Frankie Valli) -- Come together (Tina
     Turner) -- You never give me your money (Wil Malone
     and Lou Reizner) -- The end (London Symphony
     Orchestra)
     Note: This film soundtrack album includes numerous
     versions of Lennon-McCartney (Beatles) songs per-
     formed by other rock groups and artists (as listed
     above) backed by the London Symphony Orchestra or the
     Royal Philharmonic Orchestra. This Lou Reizner
     produced album reached #48 on the Billboard pop album
     chart. The album was re-released as The songs of
     John Lennon and Paul McCartney performed by the
     world's greatest rock artists (1977 20th Century
     2T-540, US).

BATT, MIKE

   586   <u>Six days in Berlin</u>. 1981 Epic FE-37665, US/ 1981
            Epic 85149, UK.

            Note: This album contains music using drums, elec-
            tric guitars, keyboards and the Berlin Opera Orches-
            tra.

   587   <u>Tarot suite</u>. 1979 Epic NJE-36312, US/ 1979 Epic
            EPC-86099, UK.

            Contents: Introduction (The journey of a fool) --
            Imbecile -- Plainsong -- Lady of the dawn -- The
            valley of swords -- Losing your way in the rain --
            Tarota -- The night of the dead -- The dead of the
            night -- Run like the wind
            Note: Mike Batt, Colin Blunstone, Roger Chapman and
            others (on guitar, sax, drums, and vocals) team with
            the London Symphony Orchestra.

   588   <u>Waves</u>. 1980 Epic EPC-84617, UK.

            Note: The Amsterdam Chamber Orchestra appears on
            this album.

BEATLES

   589   "A day in the life." <u>Sgt. Pepper's Lonely Hearts</u>
            <u>Club Band</u>. 1967 Capitol SMAS-2653, US/ 1967
            Parlophone PCS-7027, UK.

            Note: A forty-odd piece orchestra drawn from the
            London Philharmonic Orchestra appears in this song
            during the surreal breaks. The song later appeared
            as the B-side of the single "Sgt. Pepper's Lonely
            Hearts Club Band/With a little help from my friends"
            (1978 Capitol 4612, US). The song also appears on
            the Beatles' compilation <u>1967-1970</u> (1973 Apple
            [Capitol] SKBO-3404, US/ 1973 Parlophone PCSP-718,
            UK).

BEDFORD, DAVID

            <u>The orchestral tubular bells</u>. <u>See</u> Mike Oldfield

   590   <u>Star's end</u>. 1974 Virgin VR-13114, US/ 1974 Virgin
            V-2020, UK.

            Note: This album features David Bedford (on key-
            boards), Mike Oldfield (on guitar and bass guitar),
            percussion, and the Royal Philharmonic Orchestra.

CALE, JOHN

   591   <u>The academy in peril</u>. 1972 Reprise MS-2079, US/ 1972
            Reprise K-44212, UK.

Note: The Royal Philharmonic Orchestra appears on
the pieces titled "Three orchestral pieces: Faust,
The balance, Capt. Morgan's lament" and "John
Milton."

CARAVAN

592 <u>Caravan & the New Symphonia</u>. 1974 Decca PS-650, US/
      1974 Deram SKLR-1110, UK.

Contents: Introduction -- Mirror for the day --The
love in your eye -- Virgin on the ridiculous -- For
Richard
Note: This album was recorded live at the Theatre
Royal, Drury Lane, London on October 28, 1973. The
group Caravan plays guitar, bass, organ, electric
piano, synthesizer and electric viola, augmented by
the orchestra New Symphonia.

COSTELLO, ELVIS

593 <u>I'm your toy</u>. 1982 F-Beat XX21T, UK (EP).

Contents: I'm your toy -- My shoes keep walking back
to you -- Honky tonk girl -- Blues keep calling
Note: This EP was recorded live with Elvis Costello
and the Royal Philharmonic Orchestra at Royal Albert
Hall, London, on January 7, 1982.

DEEP PURPLE

594 <u>Concerto for group and orchestra</u>. 1970 Warner Bros.
      WS-1860, US/ 1970 Harvest SHVL-767, UK.

Contents: First movement: moderato, allegro, vivace
-- Second movement: pt. 1 andante, pt. 2 -- Third
movement
Note: This album was recorded live by Deep Purple
and the Royal Philharmonic Orchestra at Royal Albert
Hall, London, on September 24, 1969. The album
reached #149 on the Billboard pop album chart. Group
member Jon Lord composed the concerto, in which the
rock group and orchestra trade off riffs.

EKSEPTION

595 "Finale III." <u>Trinity</u>. 1973 Philips 6423-056,
      Netherlands.

Note: This piece features the Dutch Chamber Choir
with Ekseption.

596 "Piccadilly sweet." <u>00.04</u>. 1971 Philips 6423-019,
      Netherlands.

Note: This piece features the Royal Philharmonic
Orchestra with Ekseption.

EMERSON, LAKE & PALMER

597   Emerson, Lake & Palmer in concert. 1979 Atlantic
       SD-19255, US/ 1979 Atlantic K-50757, UK.

       Contents: Introductory fanfare -- Peter Gunn --
       Tiger in a spotlight -- C'est la vie -- The enemy
       god/Dances with the black spirits -- Knife-edge --
       Piano concerto no. 1: third movement -- Pictures at
       an exhibition
       Note: Although this orchestra was not already
       established prior to Emerson, Lake & Palmer's 1977
       tour and live album, it was a hand-picked fifty-six
       piece orchestra and six voice chorus conducted by
       Godfrey Salmon. The orchestra was used only on the
       first fifteen concert dates in 1977 until the cost
       became prohibitive and the orchestra was dropped from
       the rest of the tour. The live album was recorded at
       Olympic Stadium, Montreal, Canada.

598   "Maple leaf rag." Works, volume 2. 1977 Atlantic
       SD-19147, US/ 1977 Atlantic K-50422, UK.

       Note: Keith Emerson performs on piano with the
       London Philharmonic Orchestra.

599   "Piano concerto no. 1." Works, volume 1. 1977
       Atlantic SD2-7000, US/ 1977 Manticore K-80009, UK.

       Note: Keith Emerson performs his own composition on
       piano with the London Philharmonic Orchestra. The
       sections are titled: first movement (allegro
       giojoso), second movement (andante molto cantabile),
       third movement (toccata con fuoco).

600   "Pirates." Works, volume 1. 1977 Atlantic SD2-7000,
       US/ 1977 Manticore K-80009, UK.

       Note: Emerson, Lake & Palmer recorded this piece
       with the Orchestra de l'Opéra de Paris.

ENO, BRIAN

601   Taking Tiger Mountain by strategy. 1974 Island
       ILPS-9309, US and UK.

       Note: Brian Eno recorded with the Portsmouth
       Sinfonia, sometimes known as the "world's worst
       symphony." The album was reissued (197? Island
       1-3001, US/ 197? Polydor 2302-068, 198? Editions EG
       ENO-2, UK).

GILMOUR, DAVID

602   "Let's get metaphysical." About face. 1984 Columbia
       FC-39296, US/ 1984 Harvest SHSP-2400791, UK.

Note: The National Philharmonic Orchestra appears in this song. David Gilmour is also a member of the rock group Pink Floyd.

LORD, JON

603 Gemini suite. 1971 Capitol SMAS-870, US/ 1971 Purple
    TPSA-7501, UK.

Note: Jon Lord is assisted by other members of Deep Purple (David Coverdale, Roger Glover, Ian Paice) along with Tony Ashton, Yvonne Elliman and Albert Lee. The London Symphony Orchestra, conducted by Malcolm Arnold, appears on this recorded version of mostly instrumental music. The piece originally was performed in 1970 over the BBC by Deep Purple and the South Bank Pop Orchestra.

604 Sarabande. 1976 Hörzu 1C-062-97-943, Germany/ 1976
    Purple TPSA-7516, UK.

Contents: Fantasia -- Sarabande -- Aria -- Gigue -- Bourée -- Pavanne -- Caprice -- Finale
Note: This baroque dance suite (à la Bach) features the Philharmonia Hungarica, conducted by Eberhard Schoener, along with Jon Lord on various keyboards. Other performers add guitars and percussion. The album was recorded September 3-6, 1975 at Stadt Halle Oererckenschwick near Düsseldorf, Germany.

605 Windows. 1974 EMI Electrola 1C-062-95-634, Germany/
    1974 Purple TPSA-7513, UK.

Contents: Continuo on B.A.C.H. (realization of a well known incomplete fugue by Bach based on a scale using the notes represented by his own name B^b - A - C - $B^\#$) -- Window: first movement, second movement, third movement
Note: This album was recorded live with the Munich Chamber Opera Orchestra, conducted by Eberhard Schoener, on June 1, 1974 at the Herkulessaal of the Munich Residenz. Lord and the orchestra were supplemented by rock musicians Tony Ashton, Glenn Hughes, Peter York, Ray Fenwick and David Coverdale.

MAHAVISHNU ORCHESTRA. See McLAUGHLIN, JOHN

MANDALABAND

606 The eye of Wendor: prophechies. 1978 Chrysalis
    CHR-1181, UK.

Contents: The eye of Wendor -- Florian's song -- Ride to the city -- Almar's tower -- Like the wind -- The tempest -- Dawn of a new day -- Departure from Carthilias -- Elsethea -- Witch of Waldow Wood --

Silesandre -- AEnord's lament -- Funeral of the king
-- Coronation of Damien
Note: Mandalaband is joined on this album by members
of the Hallé Orchestra, the Gerald Brown Singers,
Justin Hayward, Eric Stewart, Graham Gouldman, Maddy
Prior, Lol Creme, and Kevin Godley.

607 Mandalaband. 1975 Chrysalis CHR-1095, UK.

Note: The London Chorale appears on this album.

McLAUGHLIN, JOHN, AND THE MAHAVISHNU ORCHESTRA

608 Apocalypse. 1974 Columbia KC-32957, US/ 1974 CBS
      69076, UK.

Contents: Power of love -- Vision is a naked sword
-- Smile of the beyond -- Wings of karma -- Hymn to
Him
Note: This jazz-rock album features the London
Symphony Orchestra, conducted by Michael Tilson
Thomas, and John McLaughlin's Mahavishnu Orchestra.

MOODY BLUES

609 Days of future passed. 1967 Deram DES-18012, US/
      1967 Deram SML-707, UK.

Contents: The day begins -- Dawn: dawn is a feeling
-- The morning: another morning -- Lunch break:
peak hour -- The afternoon: forever afternoon
(Tuesday?) -- Evening: The sunset; twilight time --
The night: nights in white satin
Note: The London Festival Orchestra, conducted by
Peter Knight, complements the members of the Moody
Blues. The album reached #3 on the Billboard pop
album chart in 1968. The single "Nights in white
satin" (1968 Deram 85023, reissued 1972, US/ 1967
Deram DM-161, UK) reached #2 on the Billboard pop
singles chart in 1972. In Britain, this single hit
the charts in 1967 (#19), 1972 (#9), and 1979 (#14).
The single "Tuesday afternoon (forever afternoon)"
(1968 Deram 85028, US) reached #24 on the Billboard
pop singles chart in 1968.

MOTHERS OF INVENTION. See ZAPPA, FRANK

NICE

610 The five bridges. 1970 Mercury SR-61295, US/ 1970
      Charisma CAS-1014, UK.

Relevant contents: [Five bridges suite]: Fantasia
(1st bridge); 2nd bridge; Chorale (3rd bridge); High
level fugue (4th bridge); Finale (5th bridge) --
Intermezzo, Karelia suite -- Pathétique symphony no.
6, 3rd mvt.

Note: The Nice recorded the above pieces with the
Sinfonia of London. The album was later reissued as
part of the double set Keith Emerson with the Nice
(1972 Mercury SRM-2-6500, US).

NITZSCHE, JACK

611 St. Giles Cripplegate. 1972 Reprise MS-2092 US/ 197?
     Harvest 2031, UK.

     Contents: #6 -- #4 (for Mori) -- #2 -- #3 -- #1 --
     #5
     Note: Jack Nitzsche recorded with the London
     Symphony Orchestra at the church St. Giles Cripple-
     gate.

OLDFIELD, MIKE

612 The orchestral tubular bells. 1975 Virgin VR-13115,
     US/ 1975 Virgin V-2026, UK.

     Note: Mike Oldfield performed a new version of his
     popular Tubular bells (see 787) this time with the
     Royal Philharmonic Orchestra, as arranged by David
     Bedford.

PALMER, CARL

613 "Concerto for percussion." recorded about 1976,
     unreleased.

     Note: This former member of Emerson, Lake & Palmer
     (now of Asia) once recorded this piece with the
     London Philharmonic Orchestra for use on a future
     solo album. On this classically tinged piece, Palmer
     plays all types of tuned percussion, including
     vibraphone and marimba.

PARSONS, ALAN, PROJECT

614 Eve. 1979 Arista AL-9504, US/ 1979 Arista SPART-
     1100, UK.

     Contents: Lucifer -- You lie down with dogs -- I'd
     rather be a man -- You won't be there -- Winding me
     up -- Damned if I do -- Don't hold back -- Secret
     garden -- If I could change your mind
     Note: The Munich Chamber Opera Orchestra appears on
     this album.

615 Eye in the sky. 1982 Arista AL-9599, US/ 1982 Arista
     3484, UK.

     Contents: Sirius -- Eye in the sky -- Children of
     the moon -- Gemini -- Silence and I -- You're gonna
     get your fingers burned -- Psychobabble -- Mammagamma
     -- Step by step -- Old and wise

Note: This album uses the English Chorale as background singers.

616   I robot. 1977 Arista AL-7002, US/ 1977 Arista
       SPARTY-1012, UK.

      Contents: I robot -- I wouldn't want to be like you
      -- Some other time -- Breakdown -- Don't let it show
      -- The voice -- Nucleus -- Day after day -- Total
      eclipse -- Genesis ch. 1, v. 32
      Note: Background singers include the English Chorale
      and the New Philharmonia Chorus. An unnamed orches-
      tra also appears on the album.

617   Tales of mystery and imagination. 1976 20th Century
       T-339, US/ 1976 Charisma CDS-4003, UK.

      Contents: A dream within a dream -- The raven -- The
      tell-tale heart -- The cask of Amontillado -- (The
      system of) Doctor Tarr and Professor Fether -- The
      fall of the house of Usher (prelude, arrival, inter-
      mezzo, pavane, fall) -- To one in paradise
      Note: The English Chorale and an unnamed orchestra
      appear on this album. It was re-released with a new
      cover (20th Century T-539 and Casablanca T-739). The
      songs are based on Edgar Allan Poe stories and poems.

618   The turn of a friendly card. 1980 Arista AL-9518,
       US/ 1980 Arista DLART-1, UK.

      Contents: May be a price to pay -- Games people play
      -- Time -- I don't wanna go home -- The gold bug --
      The turn of a friendly card -- The turn of a friendly
      card (part one) -- Snake eyes -- The ace of swords --
      Nothing left to lose -- The turn of a friendly card
      (part two)
      Note: The Munich Chamber Opera Orchestra appears on
      this album.

PINK FLOYD

619   "Atom heart mother suite." Atom heart mother. 1970
       Harvest SMAS-382, US/ 1970 Harvest SHVL-781, UK.

      Note: Pink Floyd recorded this piece with a brass
      section, small string ensemble, and the John Aldis
      Choir. As a result of this piece, Pink Floyd was
      selected in 1971 as the first rock group to play at
      the Montreux Classical Music Festival.

620   The final cut. 1983 Columbia QC-38243, US/ 1983
       Harvest SHPF-1983, UK.

      Note: The National Philharmonic Orchestra appears on
      this album and was arranged and conducted by Michael
      Kamen, formerly of New York Rock & Roll Ensemble.

621 The wall. 1979 Columbia PC2-36183, US/ 1979 Harvest
     SHDW-411, UK.

     Note: An unnamed orchestra appears on this album and
     their parts were arranged by Michael Kamen and Bob
     Ezrin. The single "Comfortably numb" (1980 Columbia
     13-02165, US) noticeably features this orchestra.

PROCOL HARUM

622 Procol Harum live. 1972 A&M SP-4335, US/ 1972
     Chrysalis CHR-1004, UK.

     Contents: Conquistador -- Whaling stories -- A salty
     dog -- All this and more -- In held 'twas in I:
     Glimpses of Nirvana, 'Twas teatime at the circus, In
     the autumn of my madness, Look to your soul, Grand
     finale
     Note: Procol Harum recorded this album live with
     the Edmonton Symphony Orchestra and the Da Camera
     Singers at Jubilee Auditorium, Edmonton, Alberta on
     November 18, 1971. The album reached #5 on the
     Billboard pop album chart. The single "Conquistador/
     A salty dog" (1972 A&M 1347, US) reached #16 on the
     Billboard pop singles chart. This version of "Con-
     quistador" also appears on Best of Procol Harum (1972
     A&M SP-4401 [3529], US).

RAINBOW

623 "Gates of Babylon." Long live rock 'n' roll. 1978
     Polydor POLD-5002 (6143), US/ 1978 Polydor 2490-
     142, UK.

     Note: The Bavarian String Ensemble appears on this
     piece.

624 Rainbow rising. 1976 Oyster OY-1-1601, US/ 1976
     Oyster 2490-137, UK.

     Note: The Munich Philharmonic Orchestra appears on
     this album.

RENAISSANCE

625 Live at Carnegie Hall. 1976 Sire SASY-3902-2 (6029),
     US/ 1976 BTM 2001, UK.

     Contents: Prologue -- Ocean gypsy -- Can you under-
     stand -- Carpet of the sun -- Running hard -- Mother
     Russia -- Scheherazade -- Ashes are burning
     Note: This double album was recorded live by the
     rock group Renaissance with members of the New York
     Philharmonic Orchestra at Carnegie Hall on June
     20-22, 1975.

626   "Song of Scheherazade." Scheherazade and other
       stories. 1975 Sire SR-6017 (SASD-7510), US/ 1975
       BTM 1006, UK.

       Note: Members of the London Symphony Orchestra
       appear on this long song, inspired by, but not based
       on, Rimsky-Korsakov. The parts of the song are:
       Fanfare, The betrayal, The sultan, Love theme, The
       young prince and princess, Festival preparations,
       Fugue for the sultan, The festival, Finale. A live
       version entitled "Scheherazade" appears on Live at
       Carnegie Hall (1976 Sire SASY-3902-2 [6029], US/ 1976
       BTM 2001, UK).

ROLLING STONES

627   "You can't always get what you want." Let it bleed.
       1969 London NPS-4, US/ 1969 Decca SKL-5025, UK
       (albums); 1969 London 910, US/ 1969 Decca F-12952,
       1973 Decca F-13404, UK (singles).

       Note: The London Bach Choir performs background
       vocals on this song. The U.S. single reached #42 on
       the Billboard pop singles chart in 1973. The 1969
       U.S. and U.K. singles were the B-sides of "Honky tonk
       women." The 1973 U.K. single was the B-side of "Sad
       day." The song also appears on the compilation Hot
       rocks: 1964-1971 (1972 London 2PS-606/607, US).

RONSTADT, LINDA

628   What's new?. 1983 Asylum 60260, US/ 1983 Asylum
       9602601, UK.

       Contents: What's new? -- I've got a crush on you --
       Guess I'll hang my tears out to dry -- Crazy he calls
       me -- Someone to watch over me -- I don't stand a
       ghost of a chance with you -- What'll I do -- Lover
       man (Oh where can you be) -- Good-bye
       Note: Although these songs are not rock, per se,
       Linda Ronstadt has been often considered a rock
       singer. She recorded these nonrock standards with
       the Nelson Riddle Orchestra. The album reached the
       top 10 on the Billboard pop album chart.

SIEGEL-SCHWALL BAND

629   Three pieces for blues band and symphony orchestra.
       1973 Deutsche Grammophon 2530-309, Germany/ 1974
       Polydor 2530-309, US.

       Note: This album was recorded June 22-24, 1972 by
       the Siegel-Schwall Band with the San Francisco
       Symphony Orchestra, conducted by Seiji Ozawa, at the

San Franciso War Memorial Opera House. The album
reached #105 on the Billboard pop album chart. A
single, "Blues band opus 50," was released (1973
Deutsche Grammophon 15068). The work, composed by
William Russo, was originally performed live with the
Corky Siegel Blues Band and the New York Philharmonic
Orchestra on October 9, 1969.

TRIUMVIRAT

630   Illusions on a double dimple. c1973, 1974 Harvest
        ST-11311, US/ 1974 Harvest SHSP-4030, UK.

      Note: The rock group Triumvirat recorded with the
      Cologne Opera House Orchestra and the Kurt Edelhagen
      Brass Section on this album.

WAKEMAN, RICK

631   Journey to the centre of the earth. 1974 A&M SP-
        3621, US/ 1974 A&M AMLH-63621, UK.

      Contents: The journey -- Recollection -- The battle
      -- The forest
      Note: Rick Wakeman (on keyboards) and other rock
      musicians (on guitars and percussion) recorded this
      album with the London Symphony Orchestra and the
      English Chamber Choir. The live recording took place
      at Royal Festival Hall, London, on January 18, 1974.
      The album reached #3 on the Billboard pop album chart
      and it was nominated in 1974 for a Grammy in the
      category of pop instrumental. The orchestra was
      conducted by David Measham and the production coordi-
      nator was Lou Reizner.

632   Lisztomania. 1975 A&M SP-4546, US/ 1975 A&M AMLH-
        64546, UK.

      Contents: Rienzi/Chopsticks fantasia -- Love's dream
      -- Dante period -- Orpheus song -- Hell -- Hiber-
      nation -- Excelsior song -- Master race -- Rape,
      pillage & clap -- Funerailles -- Free song -- Peace
      at last
      Note: Rick Wakeman and his English Rock Ensemble
      recorded this album with the National Philharmonic
      Orchestra. The contents of this film soundtrack
      album are based on Wagner and Liszt themes. Details
      are covered in part I under Rick Wakeman.

633   The myths and legends of King Arthur and the knights
        of the round table. 1975 A&M SP-4515, US/ 1975 A&M
        AMLH-64515, UK.

      Contents: Arthur -- Lady of the lake -- Guinevere --

Sir Lancelot and the Black Knight -- Merlin the
magician (pt. I-IV) -- Sir Galahad -- The last battle
Note: This album was recorded by Rick Wakeman with
the English Chamber Choir and a forty-five piece
studio orchestra conducted by David Measham of the
London Symphony Orchestra. The album reached #21 on
the Billboard pop album chart.

634   1984. 1981 Charisma CDS-4022, UK.

Contents: Wargames -- Julia -- Hymn -- Room
(Brainwash) -- Robot man -- Sorry -- No name --
Forgotten memories -- Proles -- 1984
Note: A thirty member orchestra drawn from the New
World Symphony Orchestra is joined by Rick Wakeman,
Chaka Khan, Jon Anderson, Steve Harley, and Kenny
Lynch. Rick Wakeman composed and orchestrated the
music. Tim Rice wrote the lyrics.

WAYNE, JEFF

635   The war of the worlds. 1978 Columbia PC2-35290, US/
        1978 CBS 96000, UK.

Contents: The coming of the Martians: The eve of
the war, Horsell Common and the heat ray, The artil-
leryman and the fighting machine, Forever autumn --
The earth under the Martians: The red weed pt. 1,
The spirit of man, The red weed pt. 2, Brave new
world, Dead London, Epilogue pt. 1, Epilogue pt. 2
Note: An unnamed studio orchestra is joined by rock
artists Justin Hayward, Julie Covington, David Essex,
Phil Lynott, Joe Partridge, and Chris Thompson. An
abridged version (1978 CBS 85337) and a special radio
edition (1978 Columbia AS-454) were released. Two
singles by Justin Hayward were "Eve of the war" (1978
CBS 6496, UK) and "Forever autumn" (1978 Columbia
3-10799, US/ 1978 CBS 6368, UK).

WHO

636   Tommy (orchestral version). 1972 Ode SP-99001, US/
        1972 Ode SP-88001, UK.

Contents: Overture -- It's a boy -- 1921 -- Amazing
journey -- Sparks -- Eyesight to the blind -- Christmas -- Cousin Kevin -- The acid queen -- Underture --
Do you think it's alright? -- Fiddle about -- Pinball
wizard -- There's a doctor I've found -- Go to the
mirror boy -- Tommy can you hear me? -- Smash the
mirror -- I'm free -- Miracle cure -- Sally Simpson
-- Welcome -- Tommy's holiday camp -- We're not gonna
take it -- See me, feel me
Note: This version of the rock opera Tommy, originally performed by the Who alone (see 851), is

performed on this album by the London Symphony
Orchestra and the LSO Chamber Choir with guest
soloists: Pete Townshend (narrator), Roger Daltrey
(Tommy), John Entwistle (Cousin Kevin), Sandy Denny
(nurse), Graham Bell (lover), Stevie Winwood (Tommy's
father), Maggie Bell (Tommy's mother), Richie Havens,
Merry Clayton (Acid queen), Ringo Starr (Uncle
Ernie), Rod Stewart (Pinball Wizard), Richard Harris
(doctor). The album was recorded at Olympic Studios
in London and was produced by Lou Reizner. It
reached #5 on the Billboard pop album chart. The box
set of double album and 28-page book won a 1973
Grammy award for best album package.

637   Tommy: live at the Rainbow. 1972 TAKRL 2956 (double
      bootleg album).

      Contents: same as 636, except that "Amazing
      Journey/Sparks" is combined, "Sensation" is added,
      and "See me, feel me" is deleted
      Note: This bootleg live version of Tommy by the
      London Symphony Orchestra and LSO Chamber Choir with
      guest soloists was recorded at the December 9, 1972
      Rainbow Theatre performance in London. The conductor
      was David Measham and the producer was Lou Reizner.
      The guest soloists are the same as 636 except that
      Keith Moon plays Uncle Ernie and Peter Sellers plays
      the doctor.

YOUNG, NEIL

638   "A man needs a maid." Harvest. 1972 Reprise
      RS(MS)-2032 (2277), US/ 1972 Reprise K-54005, UK.

      Note: The London Symphony Orchestra provides a
      backing track for this song. The orchestra is
      conducted by David Measham and the music was arranged
      by Jack Nitzsche.

639   "There's a world." Harvest. 1972 Reprise
      RS(MS)-2032 (2277), US/ 1972 Reprise K-54005, UK.

      Note: The London Symphony Orchestra provides a
      backing track for this song. The orchestra is
      conducted by David Measham and the music was arranged
      by Jack Nitzsche.

ZAPPA, FRANK (and the Mothers of Invention)

640   200 motels. 1971 United Artists UAS-9956, US/ 1971
      United Artists 50003, UK.

      Note: This film soundtrack album features the Royal
      Philharmonic Orchestra and Chorus with Frank Zappa
      and the Mothers of Invention.

B. Rock Groups or Artists Appearing with Orchestras
    in Live Performance before an Audience

Note: An asterisk (*) denotes a
performance available as a recorded
album (see part IIIA).

BARCLAY JAMES HARVEST

641 Barclay James Harvest/Barclay James Harvest Symphony
     Orchestra (1970) UK tour [touring orchestra]

BEDFORD, DAVID

*642 David Bedford/Royal Philharmonic Orchestra (November
      1974) London Festival Hall

BEE GEES

643 Bee Gees/touring orchestra (1968) tour

644 Bee Gees/London Symphony Orchestra (1973) Royal
     Festival Hall, London

BLOOD, SWEAT & TEARS

645 Blood, Sweat & Tears/Los Angeles Philharmonic Orches-
     tra (1970) Hollywood Bowl, Los Angeles

646 Blood, Sweat & Tears/New Orleans Orchestra
     (November 13, 1971), New Orleans

CARAVAN

*647 Caravan/New Symphonia (October 28, 1973) Theatre
      Royal, London

CHAMBERS BROTHERS

648 Chambers Brothers/New York Pro Musica Antiqua (Spring
     1968) Electric Circus, New York City [Electric
     Easter]

CIRCUS MAXIMUS

649 Circus Maximus/New York Pro Musica Antiqua (December
     26 and 30, 1967), Carnegie Hall, New York City
     [Electric Christmas]

COSTELLO, ELVIS

*650 Elvis Costello/Royal Philharmonic Orchestra
      (January 7, 1982) Royal Albert Hall, London

DEEP PURPLE

":651   Deep Purple/Royal Philharmonic Orchestra
        (September 24, 1969) Royal Albert Hall, London

  652   Deep Purple/Los Angeles Philharmonic Orchestra
        (August 25, 1970), Hollywood Bowl, Los Angeles

EKSEPTION

  653   Ekseption/Musica da Camera/Trio Louis van Dijk
        (February 26, 1970) Utrecht

ELEPHANT'S MEMORY

  654   Elephant's Memory/American Symphony Orchestra (1969)
        Carnegie Hall, New York City

EMERSON, LAKE & PALMER

":655   Emerson, Lake & Palmer/touring orchestra (1977) tour

GRATEFUL DEAD

  656   Grateful Dead/Road/Buffalo Philharmonic Orchestra
        (March 17, 1970)

LORD, JON

":657   Jon Lord/Munich Chamber Opera Orchestra (June 1,
        1974) Herkulessaal of the Munich Residenz, Munich
        [Windows]

MOTHERS OF INVENTION. See ZAPPA, FRANK

NEW YORK ROCK & ROLL ENSEMBLE

  658   New York Rock & Roll Ensemble/Baltimore Symphony

  659   New York Rock & Roll Ensemble/Concertante of the
        Symphony of New York (February 23, 1969) Phil-
        harmonic Hall, New York City

  660   New York Rock & Roll Ensemble/New York Philharmonic
        Orchestra (February 8, 1969) Philharmonic Hall, New
        York City

  661   New York Rock & Roll Ensemble/San Francisco Symphony
        (?) Hollywood Bowl, Los Angeles

NICE

  662   Nice/Royal Philharmonic Orchestra (March 6, 1970)
        London?

OLDFIELD, MIKE

 ⁚663   Mike Oldfield/Royal Philharmonic Orchestra (1975)

PROCOL HARUM

 ⁚664   Procol Harum/Edmonton Symphony Orchestra
        (November 18, 1971) Jubilee Auditorium, Edmonton,
        Alberta

RASCALS

  665   Rascals/American Symphony Orchestra (July 11, 1968),
        Garden State Arts Center, Holmdel, N.J.

RENAISSANCE

 ⁚666   Renaissance/members of New York Philharmonic Orches-
        tra (June 20-22, 1975) Carnegie Hall, New York City

SANTANA

  667   Santana/Los Angeles Philharmonic Orchestra (197?)

SIEGEL-SCHWALL BAND

  668   Corky Siegel Blues Band/New York Philharmonic Orches-
        tra (October 9, 1969) Philharmonic Hall, New York
        City

 ⁚669   Siegel-Schwall Band/San Francisco Symphony Orchestra
        (June 22-24, 1972) War Memorial Opera House, San
        Francisco

TEN WHEEL DRIVE

  670   Ten Wheel Drive/American Symphony Orchestra
        (March 14, 1971) Carnegie Hall, New York City
        [Little Big Horn rock oratorio]

WAKEMAN, RICK

 ⁚671   Rick Wakeman/London Symphony Orchestra and English
        Chamber Choir (January 18, 1974) Royal Festival
        Hall, London [Journey to the centre of the earth]

  672   Rick Wakeman/London Symphony Orchestra and English
        Chamber Choir (July 1974) open air at Crystal
        Palace, London [Journey to the centre of the earth]

  673   Rick Wakeman/touring orchestra and chorus (1974) tour

  674   Rick Wakeman/unnamed orchestra and chorus (May 30,
        1975) Wembley Empire Pool, London [ice pageant
        version of Myths and legends of King Arthur . . .]

WHO

*675 Who/London Symphony Orchestra and Chamber Choir
        (December 9, 1972) Rainbow Theatre, London

ZAPPA, FRANK (and the Mothers of Invention)

676 Frank Zappa and the Mothers of Invention/Los Angeles
       Philharmonic Orchestra (May 15, 1970) Pauley
       Pavilion, UCLA, Los Angeles

       C. Selected Examples of Rock Music Simulating
           a Baroque or Classical Sound/Structure

ABC

677 "All of my heart." Lexicon of love. 1982 Mercury
       SRM-1-4059, US/ 1982 Neutron NTRS-1, UK.

       Note: This is the most orchestral sounding piece on
       the album. A small fourteen piece orchestra supple-
       ments the rock group ABC.

AMAZING BLONDEL

678 Fantasia lindum. 1971 Island SW-9310, US/ 1971
       Island ILPS-9156, UK.

       Note: This album features an Elizabethan sound using
       lutes, recorders, harpsichord, etc.

679 "Prelude" and "The leaving of the country lover."
       Blondel. 1973 Island SW(SMAS)-9339, US/ 1973
       Island ILPS-9257, UK.

       Note: The use of strings and wind instruments lends
       a classical sound to this song sequence.

AMBROSIA

680 "Danse with me George." Somewhere I've never
       travelled. 1976 20th Century T-510, US/ 1976 20th
       Century BTH-510, UK.

       Note: This song has a distinct classical tone,
       especially the ending. The album was reissued (1978
       Warner Bros. BSK-3182, US).

APHRODITE'S CHILD

       (see also part I)

681 666. 1972 Vertigo VEL-2-500, US/ 1972 Vertigo
       6641-581 (6673-001), UK?

ARS NOVA

      (see also part I)

  682   <u>Ars Nova</u>. 1968 Elektra EKS-74020, US.

      Note: The pieces on this album which are actually
      based on classical themes are described in part I,
      but there are other songs which only sound like
      classical music, e.g., "Fields of people," "Pavan for
      my lady," "March of the mad duke's circus."

  683   <u>Sunshine and shadows</u>. 1969 Atlantic SD-8221, US/
      1969 Atlantic 588-196, UK.

ART IN AMERICA

  684   "Art in America." <u>Art in America</u>. 1983 Pavillion
      BFZ-38517, US.

ASIA

  685   <u>Asia</u>. 1982 Geffen GHS-2008, US/ 1982 Geffen GEF-
      85577, UK.

      Note: This rock group is composed of former members
      of Yes (Steve Howe, Geoff Downes), Emerson, Lake &
      Palmer (Carl Palmer, Greg Lake briefly), and King
      Crimson/U.K. (John Wetton). Both this album and the
      one below contain numerous classical and baroque
      style chord progressions and synthesized versions of
      strings, baroque-like trumpet, and harpsichord.

  686   <u>Alpha</u>. 1983 Geffen GHS-4008, US/ 1983 Geffen GEF-
      25508, UK.

ASSOCIATION

  687   "Requiem for the masses." <u>Insight out</u>. 1967 Warner
      Bros. WS-1696, US/ 1967 London MHAT-8342, UK
      (albums); 1967 Warner Bros. 7074, US (single).

      Note: "Church-like" harmonies are prominent in this
      song. The single is the B-side of "Never my love"
      and reached #100 on the Billboard pop singles chart.

BACK-BEAT PHILHARMONIC

  688   "Rock and roll symphony, parts 1 and 2." 1961 Laurie
      3092, US (single).

BARCLAY JAMES HARVEST

  689   <u>Barclay James Harvest</u>. 1970 Sire/London SES-97026,
      US/ 1970 Harvest SHVL-770, UK.

690   Octoberon. 1976 MCA MCA-2234, US/ 1976 Polydor
      2442-144, UK.

      Note: This rock group integrates orchestral strings.

BAROQUES

691   The Baroques. 1967 Chess LPS-1516, US.

      Note: Most of the songs on this album owe much to
      the influence of the baroque musical sound. The
      Baroques were from the American Midwest.

BEACH BOYS

      (see also part I)

692   "Caroline, no." Pet sounds. 1966 Capitol T-2458
      (mono), ST-2458 (stereo), US (albums); 1966 Capitol
      5610, US (single).

      Note: This Beach Boys' song features the use of a
      harpsichord. The album was reissued (1972 Reprise
      MS-2197, 1981 Capitol SN-16156, US/ 1981 Greenlight
      2002, UK). The song also appears on Good vibrations:
      best of the Beach Boys (1975 Reprise MS-2223, US/
      1975 Reprise K-52223, UK).

693   "Surf's up." Surf's up. 1971 Reprise RS-6453, US/
      1971 Stateside SSL-10313, UK (albums); 1971 Reprise
      1058, US (single).

      Note: This song, written by Brian Wilson and Van
      Dyke Parks, is lent a classical tinge both from its
      tune and use of piano. The song also appears on Good
      vibrations: best of the Beach Boys (1975 Reprise
      MS-2223, US/ 1975 Reprise K-52223, UK).

BEATLES

      (see also parts I and IIIA)

694   "Eleanor Rigby." Revolver. 1966 Capitol ST-2576,
      US/ 1966 Parlophone PCS-7009, UK (albums); 1966
      Capitol 5715, US/ 1966 Parlophone R-5493, UK
      (singles).

      Note: This song prominently features a double string
      quartet. The single reached #11 on the Billboard pop
      singles chart and is the B-side of "Yellow sub-
      marine." The song also appears on the compilation
      1962-1966 (1973 Apple [Capitol] SKBO-3403, US/ 1973
      Parlophone PCSP-717, UK).

695   "In my life." Rubber soul. 1965 Capitol ST-2442,
      US/ 1965 Parlophone PCS-3075, UK.

Note: A piano break is speeded up to sound like a harpsichord. The song also appears on the compilations 1962-1966 (1973 Apple [Capitol] SKBO-3403, US/ 1973 Parlophone PCSP-717, UK) and Love songs (1977 Capitol SKBL-11711, US/ 1977 Parlophone PCS-7211, UK).

696   "Penny Lane." Magical mystery tour. 1967 Capitol SMAL-2835, US (album); 1967 Capitol 5810, US/ 1967 Parlophone R-5570, UK (singles).

Note: Baroque-style trumpet is used in this song. The single reached #1 on the Billboard pop singles chart and was an RIAA certified million seller. The song also appears on the compilation 1967-1970 (1973 Apple [Capitol] SKBO-3404, US/ 1973 Parlophone PCSP-718, UK).

697   "She's leaving home." Sgt. Pepper's Lonely Hearts Club Band. 1967 Capitol SMAS-2653, US/ 1967 Parlophone PCS-7027, UK.

Note: Once described as similar in style to a Chopin mazurka, this song is mainly scored for harp and strings. It is also on the compilation Love songs (1977 Capitol SKBL-11711, US/ 1977 Parlophone PCS-7211, UK).

698   "Yesterday." Yesterday and today. 1966 Capitol ST-2553 (album); 1965 Capitol 5498, US/ 1976 Apple R-6013, UK (singles)

Note: A string quartet features prominently in this song. In the U.K., "Yesterday" appears on the album Help! (1965 Parlophone PCS-3071, UK). The U.S. album titled Help! lacked that song, but it was released on the later album described above. The song also appears on the compilations 1962-1966 (1973 Apple [Capitol] SKBO-3403, US/ 1973 Parlophone PCSP-717, UK) and Love songs (1977 Capitol SKBL-11711, US/ 1977 Parlophone PCS-7211, UK). The single reached #1 on the Billboard pop singles chart and was an RIAA certified million seller.

BEE GEES

699   "Holiday." Bee Gees first. 1967 Atco 33-223, US/ 1967 Polydor 583-012, UK (albums); 1967 Atco 6521, US (single).

Note: Strings lend a classical tone to this song. The single reached #16 on the Billboard pop singles chart. The song also probably appears on Best of Bee Gees (1969 Atco SD33-292, US/ 1969 Polydor 583-063, UK).

700   Odessa. 1969 Atco SD2-702, US/ 1969 Polydor 582-
      049/50, UK.

      Note: Songs on this album are performed with orches-
      tral accompaniment. The album was reissued (1976 RSO
      2674-012 [RS-1-3007], US).

BLOOD, SWEAT & TEARS

      (see also part I)

701   Child is father to the man. 1968 Columbia PC(CS)-
      9619, US/ 1968 CBS 63296, UK.

      Note: Many songs on this album feature the BS&T
      String Ensemble (8 violins, 2 violas, 2 cellos),
      lute, and organ.

702   "Symphony for the devil/Sympathy for the devil." 3.
      1970 Columbia KC-30090, US/ 1970 CBS 64024, UK.

BOOMTOWN RATS

703   "I don't like Mondays." The fine art of surfacing.
      1979 Columbia JC-36248, US/ 1979 Ensign ROX-11, UK
      (albums); 1980 Columbia 11117, US/ 1979 Ensign
      ENY-30, UK (singles).

      Note: Featuring classically tinged piano and
      strings, this song reached #73 on the Billboard pop
      singles chart. The song also appears on the compila-
      tion EP Ratrospective (1983 Columbia 5C-38591, US).

BOSTON

704   "Foreplay/Long time." Boston. 1976 Epic BL(PE)-
      34188, US/ 1976 EPC-81622, UK.

      Note: The classical-styled introduction to this
      piece occurs on the album version only.

CALE, JOHN

      (see also parts I and IIIA)

705   "Paris 1919." Paris 1919. 1973 Reprise MS-2131, US/
      1973 Reprise K-44239, UK.

      Note: Strings create an orchestral sound on this
      song.

CHICAGO

706   "Ballet for a girl in Buchannon." Chicago II. 1970
      Columbia 2G-24, US/ 1970 CBS 66233, UK.

      Note: This sequence of songs includes "Make me
      smile" and "Colour my world," among others.

707   "Elegy." Chicago III. 1971 Columbia C2-30110, US/
        1971 CBS 66260, UK.

      Note: This is a suite of pieces.

708   "An hour in the shower." Chicago III. 1971 Columbia
        C2-30110, US/ 1971 CBS 66260, UK.

      Note: This is a suite of pieces.

709   "Travel suite." Chicago III. 1971 Columbia C2-
        30110, US/ 1970 CBS 66260, UK.

      Note: This is a suite of pieces.

CHINA CRISIS

710   "Here come a raincloud." Working with fire and
        steel. 1983 Warner Bros. 1-25062, US/ 1983 Virgin
        V-2286, UK.

      Note: The scoring of this song includes oboe and
      strings along with synthesizer. A resurgence of
      orchestral strings in rock seems to be occurring in
      the mid-1980s.

CHRYSALIS

711   Definition. 1968 MGM SE-4547, US.

      Note: Instrumentation on this album includes
      strings, woodwinds, brass, and piano, in addition to
      guitars and drums.

COLOSSEUM

712   Those who are about to die salute you. 1969 Dunhill
        50062, US/ 1969 Fontana STLS-5510, UK.

713   Valentyne suite. 1969 Vertigo VO1, Bronze HELP-4
        (BRNA-214), UK.

COSTELLO, ELVIS

      (see also part IIIA)

714   "King of thieves." Punch the clock. 1983 Columbia
        FC-38897, US/ 1983 F-Beat XXLP-19, UK.

      Note: Piano and strings create a classical tone for
      this song.

CROCKER, FRANKIE

715   Disco suite. 1976 Casablanca NBLP-7031, US.

716   <u>Frankie Crocker and the Heart and Soul Orchestra</u>.
      1977 Casablanca NBLP-7050, US.

CROSBY & NASH

717   "To the last whale." <u>Wind on the water</u>. 1975 ABC
      ABCD-902, US/ 1975 Polydor 2310-428, UK.

      Note: This song consists of two segments. Fugal
      voices appear in "Critical mass" and classically
      tinged piano appears in "Wind on the water." The
      song also appears on David Crosby and Graham Nash's
      <u>Best of Crosby/Nash</u> (1978 ABC AA-1102, US/ 1978
      Polydor 2310-626, UK).

DALTREY, ROGER

718   "Oceans away." <u>Ride a rock horse</u>. 1975 MCA MCA-
      2147, US/ 1975 Polydor 2442-135, UK (albums); 1976
      MCA 40512, US (single).

      Note: Roger Daltrey, best known as lead singer of
      The Who, recorded this classically tinged song,
      written by Phillip Goodhand-Tait, on one of his solo
      albums. The song also appears on the compilation
      <u>Best bits</u> (1982 MCA MCA-5301, US/ 1981 Polydor
      2490-162, UK [U.K. album titled <u>Best of Roger
      Daltrey</u>]). <u>See also</u> Phillip Goodhand-Tait

DONOVAN

719   "Lalena." 1968 Epic 10393, US (single).

      Note: This song prominently incorporates violin,
      harp, and flute. The single reached #33 on the
      Billboard pop singles chart and was also released on
      the album <u>Donovan's greatest hits</u> (1969 Epic BXN[PE]-
      26439, US/ 1969 Pye NSPL-18283, UK).

DOORS

720   "Touch me." <u>The soft parade</u>. 1969 Elektra EKS-
      75005, US/ 1971 Elektra K-42079, UK (albums); 1968
      Elektra 45646, US (single).

      Note: The use of strings and harpsichord is featured
      on this song. The single reached #3 on the Billboard
      pop singles chart and was an RIAA certified million
      seller. It also appears on <u>13</u> (1970 Elektra EKS-
      74079, US/ 1971 Elektra K-42062, UK), <u>Best of the
      Doors</u> (1973 Elektra EQ-5035, US/ 1974 Elektra K-
      42143, UK), and <u>Greatest hits</u> (1980 Elektra 5E-515,
      US/ 1980 Elektra 52254, UK).

DREGS

   721   "Go for baroque." <u>Unsung heroes</u>. 1981 Arista
       AL-9548, US.

ECHO & THE BUNNYMEN

   722   <u>Ocean Rain</u>. 1984 Sire 1-25084, US/ 1984 Korova
       KODE-8, UK.

       Note: A small string section is included in the
       scoring of several songs on this album, e.g., "The
       killing moon" and "Ocean rain."

EKSEPTION

       (see also parts I and IIIA)

   723   "Piece for symphonic and rock group in A minor." <u>3</u>.
       1970 Philips 6413-007; 1971 Philips 6423-005,
       Netherlands.

       Note: This piece also is included on the compilation
       <u>Motive</u> (1972 Philips 6375-363).

ELECTRIC LIGHT ORCHESTRA

       (see also part I)

   724   <u>Eldorado; a symphony</u>. 1974 United Artists UA-
       LA339-G, US/ 1974 Warner Bros. K-56090, UK.

       Contents: Eldorado overture -- Can't get it out of
       my head -- Boy blue -- Laredo tornado -- Poor boy
       (The greenwood) -- Mister Kingdom -- Nobody's child
       -- Illusions in G major -- Eldorado -- Eldorado
       finale
       Note: This album reached #16 on the Billboard pop
       album chart and was later reissued (1978 Jet JZ-
       35526, US/ 1978 Jet LP-203, UK). "Boy blue" was
       released as a single (1975 United Artists 634, US)
       and also appears on the compilation <u>Olé ELO</u> (1976
       United Artists UA-LA630-G, 1978 Jet JZ-35528, US/
       1976 Jet LP-19, UK). "Can't get it out of my head"
       reached #9 on the Billboard pop singles chart (1975
       United Artists 573, US) and also appears on the
       compilations <u>Olé ELO</u> (1976 United Artists UA-LA630-G,
       1978 Jet JZ-35528, US/ 1976 Jet LP-19, UK) and <u>ELO's
       greatest hits</u> (1979 Jet FZ-36310, US/ 1979 Jet
       LX-525, UK). These songs, plus others on the album,
       feature ELO's violin and cellos.

   725   "Livin' thing." <u>A new world record</u>. 1976 United
       Artists UA-LA679-G, US/ 1976 Jet 30034, UK
       (albums); 1976 United Artists 888 (1177), US
       (single).

Note: ELO's string section graces this song. The single reached #13 on the Billboard pop singles chart. The album was reissued (1978 Jet JZ-35529, US/ 1978 Jet LP-200, UK). The song also appears on ELO's greatest hits (1979 Jet FZ-36310, US/ 1979 Jet LX-525, UK).

726   "Rockaria!" A new world record. 1976 United Artists UA-LA679-G, US/ 1976 Jet 30034, UK (albums); 1976 Jet UP-36209, UK (single).

Note: This song features a female opera singer performing opera-like background vocals. The lyrics of the song also mention several opera composers. The album was reissued (1978 Jet JZ-35529, US/ 1978 Jet LP-200, UK). The song also appears on ELO's greatest hits (1979 Jet FZ-36310, US/ 1979 Jet LX-525, UK).

727   "10538 overture." Electric Light Orchestra. 1971 United Artists UAS-5573, US/ 1971 Harvest SHVL-797, UK (albums); 1972 United Artists 50914, US/ 1972 Harvest HAR-5053, UK (singles).

Note: The album was reissued as No answer (1972 United Artists UAS-5573, 1978 Jet JZ-35524, US). The song also appears on Olé ELO (1976 United Artists UA-LA630-G, 1978 Jet JZ-35528, US/ 1976 Jet LP-19, UK). The single was reissued as the B-side of "Evil woman" (1975 United Artists 729, US).

ELECTRIC PRUNES

728   Mass in F minor. 1967 Reprise RS-6275, US/ 1972 Reprise K-34003, UK.

Contents: Kyrie Eleison -- Gloria -- Credo -- Sanctus -- Benedictus -- Agnus Dei
Note: This album was composed by David Axelrod, following the sequence of masses of Beethoven and Mozart. The album was reissued (1974 Reprise/WEA MID-K34003). A promotional single of "Sanctus/Credo" was released (1967 Reprise PRO-277).

EMERSON, LAKE & PALMER

(see also parts I and IIIA)

729   "Fugue." Trilogy. 1972 Cotillion SD-9903, Atlantic SD-19123, US/ 1972 Island ILPS-9186, 1973 Manticore K-43505, UK.

Note: This is a fugue-like instrumental.

730   "The three fates: Clotho, Lachesis, Atropos." Emerson, Lake & Palmer. 1971 Cotillion SD-9040,

Atlantic SD-19120, US/ 1970 Island ILPS-9132, 1973
Manticore K-43503, UK.

Note: This sequence includes performances on the
Royal Festival Hall organ and on piano. Keith
Emerson (on keyboards) formed Emerson, Lake & Palmer
after leaving the Nice. After the break-up of
Emerson, Lake, & Palmer, Carl Palmer joined the group
Asia and Greg Lake also joined Asia for a brief time
in the absence of John Wetton.

EROC

731   Eroc. 1975 Brain 1069, Germany/ 1977 Brain 201-109,
      UK.

Note: This is a German rock band which incorporates
the use of keyboards and violin.

ESPERANTO

(see also part I)

732   Esperanto Rock Orchestra. 1973 A&M SP-4399, US/ 1973
      A&M AMLH-68175, UK.

Note: In addition to rock instruments (guitar, bass,
drums, etc.), this group features a four piece string
section (violins, viola, cello).

733   Danse macabre. 1974 A&M SP-3624, US/ 1974 A&M
      AMLH-63624, UK.

Note: This album was once described as a combination
of "Gregorian chant, hard rock, and viola riffs."
The album was produced by Pete Sinfield.

FAITHFULL, MARIANNE

734   "As tears go by." Marianne Faithfull. 1965 London
      PS-423, US/ 1965 Decca LK-4689, UK (albums); 1964
      London 9697, US/ 1964 Decca F-11923, UK (singles).

Note: This song, composed by Jagger/Richards, was
also later recorded by the Rolling Stones (see 807).
Faithfull's version featured harpsichord and string
ensemble. Her version was also included on her album
Greatest hits (196? London PS-547, US/ 196? Decca
LK-?, UK). The single reached #22 on the Billboard
pop singles chart.

FOCUS

735   "Hamburger concerto." Hamburger concerto. 1974 Atco
      SD36-100, US/ 1974 Polydor 2442-124, UK.

736 "Hocus pocus." Moving waves. 1971 Sire SAS-7401,
     US/ 1971 Blue Horizon (Polydor) 2931-002, UK
     (albums); 1973 Sire 704, US/ 1972 Polydor 2001-211,
     UK (singles).

     Note: This instrumental has a distinct classical
     tone. Group leader, Thijs van Leer, studied at the
     Amsterdam Conservatoire before forming this Dutch
     rock group. The single of this instrumental reached
     #9 on the Billboard pop singles chart. The piece
     also appears on the compilation Dutch masters (1975
     Sire SASD-7505, US) and live on Live at the Rainbow
     (1973 Sire SAS-7408, US/ 1973 Polydor 2443-118, UK).

GENESIS

737 "Eleventh Earl of Mar." Wind & wuthering. 1976 Atco
     SD36-144, US/ 1977 Charisma CDS-4005, UK.

738 "The musical box." Nursery cryme. 1971 Charisma
     CAS-1052, US and UK.

     Note: The album on which this piece occurs was
     reissued (197? Atlantic 80030-1-B, 197? Charisma
     CA-2-2701, US). The piece also appears on Genesis
     live (1973 Charisma 1066, 1974 Buddah CAS-1666, US/
     1973 Charisma CLASS-1, UK), and its closing section
     on the live album Seconds out (1977 Atlantic SD2-
     9002, US/ 1977 Charisma GE-2001, UK).

739 "One for the vine." Wind & wuthering. 1976 Atco
     SD36-144, US/ 1977 Charisma CDS-4005, UK.

GENTLE GIANT

740 Gentle Giant. 1970 Vertigo 6360-020, UK.

741 Three friends. 1972 Columbia PC-31649, US/ 1972
     Vertigo 6360-070, UK.

GOODHAND-TAIT, PHILLIP

742 "Oceans away." Oceans away. 1976 Chrysalis CHR-
     1113, US and UK.

     See also Roger Daltrey

HARRIS, RICHARD

743 "MacArthur Park." A tramp shining. 1968 Dunhill
     DS-50032, US (album); 1968 Dunhill 4134, US/ 1968
     RCA 1699, UK (singles).

     Note: This unusually long classically tinged single
     reached #2 on the Billboard pop singles chart.

ILLUSION

744   <u>Out of the mist</u>. 1977 Island ILPS-9489, US and UK.

      Note: Some members of this group were previously in
      the original line-up of Renaissance that existed
      prior to 1972.

IT'S A BEAUTIFUL DAY

745   <u>It's a Beautiful Day</u>. 1969 Columbia PC(CS)-9768, US/
      1969 CBS 63722, UK.

      Note: Electric violin is the most prominent feature
      of much of this group's work. The best known song on
      this album is "White bird."

JADE WARRIOR

746   <u>Kites</u>. 1976 Island ILPS-9393, US and UK.

747   <u>Waves</u>. 1975 Island ILPS-9318, US and UK.

JETHRO TULL

      (see also part I)

748   <u>Minstrel in the gallery</u>. 1975 Chrysalsis CHR-1082,
      US and UK.

      Note: This album used a studio orchestra as a
      backing to the rock group Jethro Tull. The album
      reached #7 on the Billboard pop album chart.

749   <u>A passion play</u>. 1973 Chrysalis CHR-1040, US and UK.

      Note: Once described as "rock chamber music," this
      album reached #1 on the Billboard pop album chart.

750   <u>War child</u>. 1974 Chrysalis CHR-1067, US and UK.

      Note: This partially orchestrated album reached #2
      on the Billboard pop album chart.

JOHN, ELTON

751   "Funeral for a friend/Love lies bleeding." <u>Goodbye
      yellow brick road</u>. 1973 MCA MCA2-10003, US/ 1973
      DJM DJLPD-1001, UK.

752   "Someone saved my life tonight." <u>Captain Fantastic
      and the brown dirt cowboy</u>. 1975 MCA MCA-2142
      (3009), 1980 MCA MCA-37066, US/ 1975 DJM DJLPX-1,
      UK (albums); 1975 MCA 40421, US/ 1975 DJM DJS-385,
      UK (singles).

Note: The single reached #4 on the Billboard pop
singles chart. The song also appears on Elton John's
Greatest hits volume II (1977 MCA MCA-3027, US/ 1977
DJM DJH-20520, UK).

753 "Sorry seems to be the hardest word." Blue moves.
1976 MCA MCA2-11004, US/ 1976 Rocket ROLL-12, UK
(albums); 1976 MCA 40645, US/ 1976 Rocket ROKN-517,
UK (singles).

Note: The single reached #6 on the Billboard pop
singles chart. The song also appears on Elton John's
Greatest hits volume II (1977 MCA MCA-3027, US/ 1977
DJM DJH-20520, UK).

JON & VANGELIS

754 "Polonaise." Private collection. 1983 Polydor
813-174-1-Y-1, US/ 1983 Polydor POLH-4-813-714-2,
UK.

Note: This piece is reminiscent of the classical
polonaise. Jon Anderson, a member of Yes, and
Vangelis, once with Aphrodite's Child, perform as a
duo on this album.

KANSAS

755 Leftoverture. 1976 Kirshner JZ-34224, US/ 1976
Kirshner 81728, UK.

Note: Much of this album shows classical flourishes
and features prominent violin parts.

KAYAK

756 "Daphne." Phantom of the night. 1978 Janus JXS-
7039, US.

757 "Nothingness." Starlight dancer. 1977 Janus JXS-
7034, US/ 1977 Vertigo 6360-856, UK.

Note: This rock group is from the Netherlands.

KING CRIMSON

758 In the court of the Crimson King. 1969 Atlantic
SD-8245 (SD-19155), US/ 1969 Island ILPS-9111, UK.

Note: This album reached #28 on the Billboard pop
album chart. The most representative pieces on the
album are "The court of the Crimson King" (single:
1970 Atlantic 2703, US), "I talk to the wind," and
"Epitaph." Vocals are by Greg Lake on this album.
King Crimson proved to be a training ground for
members of later classical rock groups. The following rock artists, each at one time recording with

King Crimson, later joined the classical rock/art
rock groups in parentheses after their names: Greg
Lake (Emerson, Lake & Palmer; briefly Asia), Bill
Bruford (Yes; U.K.), John Wetton (U.K.; Asia), Jon
Anderson (Yes), Eddie Jobson (Roxy Music; U.K.;
Jethro Tull), Pete Sinfield (producer and/or lyricist
for early Roxy Music; Emerson, Lake & Palmer; P.F.M.;
and Esperanto).

759   Islands. 1971 Atlantic SD-7212, US/ 1971 Island
      ILPS-9175, UK.

      Note: This album reached #76 on the Billboard pop
      album chart. Representative pieces are "Prelude:
      song of the gulls" and "Islands."

KINKS

760   "Village green." Village Green Preservation Society.
      1968 Reprise RS-6327, US/ 1968 Pye NSPL-18233, UK.

      Note: This song incorporates harpsichord and oboe.

LED ZEPPELIN

761   "The rain song." Houses of the holy. 1973 Atlantic
      SD-7255 (SD-19130), US/ 1973 Atlantic K-50014, UK.

      Note: Strings are used in this song.

762   "Stairway to heaven." IV. 1971 Atlantic SD-7208
      (SD-19129), US/ 1971 Atlantic 2401012 (K-50008),
      UK.

      Note: This famous song by Led Zeppelin was never
      released as a single. It is partly acoustic in
      nature and features recorder accompaniment on this
      album.

LEFT BANKE

763   "Pretty ballerina." Walk away Renée. 1967 Smash
      MGS-27088 (mono), SRS-67088 (stereo), US (albums);
      1967 Smash 2074, US (single).

      Note: The single reached #15 on the Billboard pop
      singles chart. The song features piano and a string
      quartet.

764   "Walk away Renée." Walk away Renée. 1967 Smash
      MGS-27088 (mono), SRS-67088 (stereo), US (albums);
      1966 Smash 2041, US (single).

      Note: This single reached #5 on the Billboard pop
      singles chart. The song features harpsichord and a
      string quartet.

LIGHTHOUSE

765 Lighthouse. 1969 RCA LSP-4173, US.

Note: This group incorporated violin, viola and cello into their early albums.

766 Peacing it all together. 1970 RCA LSP-4225, US/ 1970 RCA SF-8121, UK.

767 Suite feeling. 1970 RCA LSP-4241, US/ 1970 RCA SF-8103, UK.

LITTLE RIVER BAND

768 "It's a long way there." Little River Band. 1975 Harvest ST-11512, US/ 1975 EMI EMC-3144, UK (albums); 1976 Harvest 4318, US (single).

Note: The single reached #28 on the Billboard pop singles chart.

LLOYD-WEBBER, ANDREW

(see also part I)

769 Jesus Christ superstar: a rock opera. 1970 Decca DXSA-7206, US.

Note: This early rock opera featured rock singers Ian Gillan (of Deep Purple), Yvonne Elliman, and Murray Head along with rock musicians and an eighty-five piece studio orchestra. The album was later reissued (1973 MCA MCA2-10000, US). Andrew Lloyd-Webber's music and Tim Rice's lyrics were also transformed into a Broadway show (1971 MCA DL7-1503, US) and a film soundtrack (1973 MCA MCA2-11000, US). The original studio recording reached #1 on the Billboard pop album chart and was nominated in 1971 for a Grammy as album of the year. Popular singles released from the original studio album were Yvonne Elliman's "I don't know how to love Him" (1971 Decca 32785 [MCA 60124], US) and Murray Head's "Superstar" (1970 Decca 32603 [MCA 60111], US). The latter was nominated for a 1971 Grammy in the category of pop vocal.

770 Joseph and the amazing technicolor dreamcoat. 1969 Decca LC-50019, US.

Note: This Andrew Lloyd-Webber/Tim Rice collaboration, a rock cantata, was also released in a Broadway version (1974 MCA MCA-399, 1982 Chrysalis CHR-1387, US). The original album reached #84 on the Billboard pop album chart in 1971.

LOVE UNLIMITED ORCHESTRA

771 "Love's theme." Rhapsody in white. 1974 20th
     Century T-433, US (album); 1973 20th Century 2069,
     US/ 1973 Pye International 7N-25635, UK (singles).

     Note: Barry White's Love Unlimited Orchestra
     released the single in December 1973. It reached #1
     on the Billboard pop singles chart and was an RIAA
     certified million seller. This instrumental incor-
     porates strings, winds, keyboards, horns, guitars,
     and a rhythm section.

LOVIN' SPOONFUL

772 "Rain on the roof." Hums of the Lovin' Spoonful.
     1966 Kama Sutra KLPS-8054, US/ 1966 Kama Sutra 401,
     UK (albums); 1966 Kama Sutra 216, US (single).

     Note: The single reached #10 on the Billboard pop
     singles chart. The song, with its harpsichord-like
     guitars, also appears on The best of the Lovin'
     Spoonful, volume II (1968 Kama Sutra KLPS-8064, US/
     1968 Kama Sutra 405, UK), The very best of the Lovin'
     Spoonful (19?? Kama Sutra KSBS-2013, US) and The best
     (1976 Kama Sutra KSBS-2608, US).

MAURIAT, PAUL

773 "L'amour est bleu (Love is blue)." Blooming hits.
     1968 Philips PHS-600-248, US (album); 1968 Philips
     40495, US/ 1968 Philips BF-1637, UK (singles).

     Note: This instrumental reached #1 on the Billboard
     pop singles chart and was an RIAA certified million
     seller.

MILES, JOHN

774 "Music." Rebel. 1976 London PS-669, US/ 1976 Decca
     SKL-5231, UK (albums); 1976 London 20086, US/ 1976
     Decca F-13627, UK (singles).

     Note: The single reached #88 on the Billboard pop
     singles chart. Orchestration is by Andrew Powell.

775 "Pull the damn thing down." Rebel. 1976 London
     PS-669, US/ 1976 Decca SKL-5231, UK.

MOODY BLUES

     (see also part IIIA)

776 In search of the lost chord. 1968 Deram DES-18017,
     US/ 1968 Deram SML-717, UK.

Note: This album reached #23 on the Billboard pop album chart.

777   On the threshold of a dream. 1969 Deram DES-18025, US/ 1969 Deram SML-1035, UK.

Note: This album reached #20 on the Billboard pop album chart.

MORRISON, VAN

778   "Everyone." Moondance. 1970 Warner Bros. WS-1835 (BSK-3103), US/ 1970 Warner Bros. K-46040, UK.

Note: Clavinette and flute appear in this song.

NEON PHILHARMONIC

779   "Morning girl." The moth confesses: a phonograph opera. 1969 Warner Bros. WS-1769, US (album); 1969 Warner Bros. 7261, US (single).

Note: The single reached #17 on the Billboard pop singles chart. The chamber-sized orchestra is composed of members usually performing with the Nashville Symphony Orchestra.

NEW SOCIETY

780   The barock sound of the New Society. 1966 RCA Victor LPM-3676 (mono), LSP-3676 (stereo), US.

Contents: Dawn of sorrow -- Of you -- Methinks thou doth protest too much -- The good times -- Paradox of love -- Child of summer -- Love thee till I die (All the king's horses) -- Long live our love -- Words of a fool -- Jamie -- (I prithee) Do not ask for love -- We have so little time
Note: This album features original baroque-style rock music. Singles were released for "Dawn of sorrow" (1966 RCA 47-8958, US) and "Do not ask for love" (1966 RCA 47-8807, US). This combination of the beat of the '60s and the Elizabethan was, in part, arranged by Jack Nitzsche.

NEW YORK ROCK & ROLL ENSEMBLE

(see also part I)

781   "Beside you." Roll over. 1971 Columbia C-30033, US/ 1971 CBS 64126, UK (albums); 1971 Columbia 45288, US (single).

NICE

(see also parts I and IIIA)

782   "Ars longa vita brevis." <u>Ars longa vita brevis</u>.
      1969 Immediate Z12-52020, US/ 1968 Immediate
      IMSP-020, UK.

      Note: The parts of this suite are titled: Prelude,
      1st movement (Awakening), 2nd movement (Realization),
      3rd movement (Acceptance "Brandenburger"), 4th
      movement (Denial), Coda (Extension to the big note).
      The album was reissued (1973 Columbia P-11634, US/
      1978 Charly CR-300019, UK). The movements "Accep-
      tance 'Brandenburger'" and "Denial" also appear on
      <u>Greatest hits</u> (1977 Immediate IML-2003, UK).

NILSSON (Harry Nilsson)

783   "Spaceman." <u>Son of Schmilsson</u>. 1972 RCA Victor
      LSP-4717, US (album); 1972 RCA 0788, US (single).

      Note: The single reached #23 on the Billboard pop
      singles chart. The song also appears on <u>Greatest
      hits</u> (1978 RCA Victor AFL1-2798, US).

784   "Without you." <u>Nilsson Schmilsson</u>. 1971 RCA Victor
      LSP-4515, US (album); 1971 RCA 0604, US/ 1971 RCA
      2165, UK (singles).

      Note: The single reached #1 on the Billboard pop
      singles chart and was an RIAA certified million
      seller. The song also appears on <u>Greatest hits</u> (1978
      RCA Victor AFL1-2798, US).

OLDFIELD, MIKE

      (see also part IIIA)

785   <u>Hergest Ridge</u>. 1974 Virgin VR-13109, US/ 1974 Virgin
      V-2013, UK.

786   <u>Ommadawn</u>. 1975 Virgin AL(PZ)-33913, US/ 1975 Virgin
      V-2043, UK.

      Note: This album has been described as a "rock
      symphonic style."

787   <u>Tubular bells</u>. 1973 Virgin VR-13105 (VA-13135;
      PE[PZ]-34116), US/ 1973 Virgin V-2001, UK.

      Note: This album reached #3 on the Billboard pop
      album chart. A single titled "Tubular bells (theme
      from film <u>The Exorcist</u>)" was released (1974 Virgin
      55100, US) and reached #7 on the Billboard pop
      singles chart due to the popularity of the film. An
      orchestral version of <u>Tubular bells</u> was released in
      1975 (see 612). A live version of "Tubular bells,
      part 1" appears on <u>Airborn</u> (1980 Virgin VA-13143,
      US).

ORCHESTRAL MANOEUVRES IN THE DARK

788   "Joan of Arc (Maid of Orleans)." Architecture &
        morality. 1981 Virgin ARE-37721, US/ 1981 Dindisc
        DID-12, UK.

        Note: This group uses string-like synthesizer
        sounds.

P.F.M. (Premiata Forneria Marconi)

789   Chocolate kings. 1976 Asylum 7E-1071, US/ 1976
        Manticore K-53508, UK.

790   Photos of ghosts. 1973 Manticore MC-66668, US/ 1973
        Manticore KK-43502, UK.

        Note: This Italian rock group is produced by Pete
        Sinfield on this album.

PARKS, VAN DYKE

        (see also part I)

791   Song cycle. 1968 Warner Bros. WS-1727, US.

        Note: This album uses the classical device of the
        song cycle and shows influences of Debussy,
        Beethoven, Mahler, Stravinsky, and Ives.

PARZIVAL

792   Legend. 1971 Teldec 14635, Germany.

        Note: This German rock group incorporates violin,
        cello, and viola on this album.

PASSPORT

793   "Piece for rock orchestra." Blue tattoo. 1981
        Atlantic SD-19304, US.

PHILLIPS, ANTHONY

794   Antiques. 1983 RCA INTS-5228, UK.

        Note: Anthony Phillips was in the very early line-up
        of Genesis at one time. This album includes pieces
        titled "Hurlingham suite," "Suite in D minor" and
        "Elegy."

795   The geese and the ghost. 1977 Passport PP-98020, US/
        1977 Hit and Run 001, UK.

PINK FLOYD

(see also part IIIA)

796 Ummagumma. 1969 Harvest STBB-388, US/ 1969 Harvest
      SHDW 1/2, UK.

     Note: An interesting piece on this album is
     "Grantchester meadows," among others. The album
     reached #74 on the Billboard pop album chart.

797 Dark side of the moon. 1973 Harvest SMAS-11163, US/
      1973 Harvest SHVL-804, UK.

     Note: This song cycle is an audiophile's dream.
     Great care was taken in production, especially by
     engineer Alan Parsons. The album reached #1 on the
     Billboard pop album chart and remained on the chart
     at some number or other for over 400 weeks. A
     half-speed mastered version was released (19?? Mobile
     MFSL-1017, US).

POCO

798 "Crazy eyes." Crazy eyes. 1973 Epic PE(KE)-32354,
      US/ 1973 Epic 65631, UK.

     Note: This song also appears on Poco's The songs of
     Richie Furay (1979 Epic JE-36211, US), a compilation.

PRATT, ANDY

799 Resolution. 1976 Nemperor NE-438, US/ 1976 Nemperor
      K-50279, UK.

     Note: It has been said that this album shows a
     Scriabin influence.

PREMIATA FORNERIA MARCONI. See P.F.M.

PROCOL HARUM

(see also parts I and IIIA)

800 "A salty dog." A salty dog. 1969 A&M SP-4179, US/
      1969 Regal Zonophone SLRZ-1009, UK (albums); 1969
      A&M 1069, US (single).

     Note: This song, once described as a classical art
     song, also appears on Best of Procol Harum (1972 A&M
     SP-4401 [3529], US). A version recorded with the
     Edmonton Symphony was also recorded (see 622).

801 "Wreck of the Hesperus." A salty dog. 1969 A&M
      SP-4179, US/ 1969 Regal Zonophone SLRZ-1009, UK.

QUEEN

802 "Bohemian rhapsody." <u>A night at the opera</u>. 1975
       Elektra 7E-1053, US/ 1975 EMI EMTC-103, UK
       (albums); 1975 Elektra 45297, US/ 1975 EMI 2375, UK
       (singles).

     Note: This opera-influenced song reached #9 on the
     Billboard pop singles chart in 1976 and was an RIAA
     certified million seller. It also appears on
     <u>Greatest hits</u> (1981 Elektra 5E-564, US/ 1981 EMI
     TV-30, UK) and live on <u>Live killers</u> (1979 Elektra
     BB-702, US/ 1979 EMI EMSP-330, UK).

RAINBOW

     (see also parts I and IIIA)

803 "Can't let you go." <u>Bent out of shape</u>. 1983 Mercury
       815-305-1M-1, US/ 1983 Polydor POLD-5116, UK.

     Note: This song has a Bach-like organ introduction.

RENAISSANCE

     (see also parts I and IIIA)

804 "Mother Russia." <u>Turn of the cards</u>. 1974 Sire
       SR-6015 (SAS-7502), US/ 1975 BTM 1000, UK.

     Note: This song shows a Shostakovich-like style. A
     live version appears on <u>Live at Carnegie Hall</u> (1976
     Sire SASY-3902-2 [6029], US/ 1976 BTM 2001, UK).

805 <u>Prologue</u>. 1972 Capitol SMAS-11116, US/ 1972
       Sovereign 7253, UK.

     Note: This album was reissued as part of the double
     set <u>In the beginning</u> (197? Capitol SWBC-11871, US).

ROCKESTRA

806 <u>Concerts for the people of Kampuchea</u>. 1981 Atlantic
       SD2-7005, US/ 1981 Atlantic K-60153, UK.

     Note: This "rock orchestra," dubbed Rockestra,
     included famous rock guitarists (e.g. Paul McCartney,
     Peter Townshend, Robert Plant, James Honeyman-Scott,
     Dave Edmunds) in lieu of string players, supplemented
     by keyboards and drums. This group performed
     "Lucille" and "Rockestra theme" at the December 1979
     benefit concerts.

ROLLING STONES

     (see also parts I and IIIA)

807 "As tears go by." December's children. 1965 London
     PS-451, US (album); 1965 London 9808, US/ 1965
     Decca F-12331, UK (singles).

     Note: Featuring a string quartet, this song reached
     #6 on the Billboard pop singles chart. The U.K.
     single was the B-side of "19th nervous breakdown."
     Marianne Faithfull released a version of this Jagger/
     Richards song in 1964 (see 734). The Rolling Stones'
     version also appears on the compilations Big hits
     (high tide and green grass) (1966 London NPS-1, US/
     1966 Decca TXS-101, UK) and Hot rocks: 1964-1971
     (1972 London 2PS-606/607, US).

808 "Dandelion." 1967 London 905, US/ 1967 Decca
     F-12654, UK (singles).

     Note: A harpsichord-like sound graces this single,
     which reached #14 on the Billboard pop singles chart.
     It also appears on the compilations Through the past
     darkly (big hits, vol. 2) (1969 London NPS-3, US/
     1969 Decca SKL-5019, UK) and More hot rocks (1972
     London 2PS-626/627, US).

809 "Lady Jane." Aftermath. 1966 London PS-476, US/
     1966 Decca SKL-4786, UK (albums); 1966 London 902,
     US (single).

     Note: Harpsichord and dulcimer were incorporaetd
     into this song. The single reached #24 on the
     Billboard pop singles chart and was the B-side of
     "Mother's little helper." The song also appears on
     the compilation More hot rocks (1972 London 2PS-
     626/627, US).

810 "Ruby Tuesday." Between the buttons. 1967 London
     PS-499, US (album); 1967 London 904, US/ 1967 Decca
     F-12546, UK (singles).

     Note: Featuring recorder, piano, and cello, this
     song reached #1 on the Billboard pop singles chart
     and was an RIAA certified million seller. The song
     also appears onthe compilations Through the past
     darkly (big hits, vol. 2) (1969 London NPS-3, US/
     1969 Decca SKL-5019, UK) and Hot rocks: 1964-1971
     (1972 London 2PS-606/607, US).

811 "She's a rainbow." Their satanic majesties request.
     1967 London NPS-2, US/ 1967 Decca TXS-103, UK
     (albums); 1967 London 906, US (single).

     Note: The single reached #25 on the Billboard pop
     singles chart. The song also appears on the compila-
     tions Through the past darkly (big hits, vol. 2)
     (1969 London NPS-3, US/ 1969 Decca SKL-5019, UK) and
     More hot rocks (1972 London 2PS-626/627, US).

RONSTADT, LINDA. <u>See</u> STONE PONEYS

ROXY MUSIC

812 "Triptych." <u>Country life</u>. 1974 Atco SD36-106, US/
1974 Island ILPS-9303, UK.

Note: Harpsichord-like keyboards are featured in this
classically tinged song.

RUSH

813 <u>A farewell to kings</u>. 1977 Mercury SRM-1-1184, US/
1977 Mercury 9100-042, UK.

814 "2112." <u>2112</u>. 1976 Mercury SRM-1-1079, US/ 1976
Mercury 9100-039, UK.

Note: The classically influenced structure of this
piece includes an "Overture" and a "Grand finale."

RUTHERFORD, MIKE

815 <u>Smallcreep's day</u>. 1980 Passport PB-9843, US/ 1980
Charisma CAS-1149, UK.

Note: Mike Rutherford is a member of Genesis.

SAGA

816 "Don't be late." <u>Silent knight</u>. 1980 Polydor (Maze)
2374-166, Canada?

SOFT MACHINE

817 <u>Third</u>. 1970 Columbia CG-30339, US/ 1970 CBS 66246,
UK.

Note: Soft Machine was the first rock group to
appear at the London "Proms" (popular classical
concerts) on August 13, 1970 at Royal Albert Hall.

SPANKY AND OUR GANG

818 "Sunday will never be the same." <u>Spanky and Our
Gang</u>. 1967 Mercury SR-61124, US/ 1967 Mercury
SMCL-20114, UK (albums); 1967 Mercury 72679, US
(single).

Note: This song incorporates strings and harpsichord. The single reached #9 on the Billboard pop
singles chart. It also appears on <u>Spanky's greatest
hits</u> (1970 Mercury SR-61227, US).

SQUEEZE

819   "Vanity fair." East side story. 1981 A&M SP-4854,
       US/ 1981 A&M AMLH-64854, UK.

      Note: This song features winds, violins, and cello.

STARCASTLE

820   Starcastle. 1976 Epic PE-33914, US/ 1976 Epic 81347,
       UK.

STEVENS, CAT

821   "Foreigner suite." Foreigner. 1973 A&M SP-4391, US/
       1973 Island ILPS-9240, UK.

      Note: This long piece is structured in a suite
      format.

822   "Sad Lisa." Tea for the tillerman. 1971 A&M SP-
       4280, US/ 1971 Island ILPS-9135, UK.

      Note: Piano, strings, and violin are prominent in
      this song.

823   "Silent sunlight." Catch bull at four. 1972 A&M
       SP-4365, US/ 1972 Island ILPS-9206, UK (albums);
       1973 A&M 1418, US (single).

      Note: The single is the B-side of "The hurt." The
      song incorporates recorder and strings.

STEWART, AL

824   "Bedsitter images." Bedsitter images. 1967 CBS
       63087 (64023), UK.

      Note: This piece also appears on the compilation The
      early years (1977 Janus 2JXS-7026, US/ 1978 RCA
      PL-25131, UK).

STONE PONEYS (featuring Linda Ronstadt)

825   "Different drum." Evergreen vol. 2. 1967 Capitol
       ST-2763, US (album); 1967 Capitol 2004 (6185), US
       (single).

      Note: This song, featuring harpsichord and string
      quartet, reached #13 on the Billboard pop singles
      chart. The song also appears on the Linda Ronstadt
      compilations Different drum (1974 Capitol ST-11269,
      US/ 1975 Capitol VMP-1010, UK) and Greatest hits
      (1976 Asylum 6E-106 [7E-1092], US/ 1976 Asylum
      K-53055, UK).

STRAWBS

826   "Autumn." Hero and heroine. 1974 A&M SP-3607, US/
       1974 A&M AMLH-63607, UK.

       Note: This song also appears on The best of Strawbs
       (1978 A&M SP-6005, US/ 1978 A&M AMLM-66005, UK.

827   From the witchwood. 1971 A&M SP-4304, US/ 1971 A&M
       AMLS-64304, UK.

       Note: Rick Wakeman performed on keyboards for this
       album. He later joined the rock group Yes for a
       time, as well as recording solo work.

828   Ghosts. 1975 A&M SP-4506, US/ 1975 A&M AMLH-68277,
       UK.

       Note: Cello is featured on this album, which reached
       #47 on the Billboard pop album chart.

SUPERTRAMP

829   "Fool's overture." Even in the quietest moments.
       1977 A&M SP-4634, US/ 1977 A&M AMLK-64634, UK.

830   "A soapbox opera." Crisis? What crisis?. 1975 A&M
       SP-4560, US/ 1975 A&M AMLH-68347, UK.

       Note: Both the above songs appear live on Paris
       (1980 A&M SP-6702, US/1980 A&M AMLM-66702, UK).

SUPREMES

       (see also part I)

831   "I hear a symphony." I hear a symphony. 1966 Motown
       MS-643, US/ 1966 Tamla STML-11028, UK (albums);
       1965 Motown 1083, US (single).

       Note: A hint of symphonic style is imparted to this
       song by strings and piano mixed into the backing
       track. The single reached #1 on the Billboard pop
       singles chart. The song also appears on Diana Ross &
       the Supremes' Anthology (1974 Motown M9-794A3, US/
       1974 Tamla TMSP-6001, UK).

SYMPHONIC METAMORPHOSIS

832   Symphonic Metamorphosis. 1970 London PS-573, US.
       Note: This album features rock music devised by
       several members of the Detroit Symphony.

SYMPHONIC SLAM

833   Symphonic Slam. 1976 A&M SP-4619, US/ 1976 A&M
       AMLH-69023, UK.

Note: An important element of this album is the polyphonic guitar synthesizer.

SYNERGY

834   <u>Electronic realizations for rock orchestra</u>. 1975 Passport PPSD-98009, US/ 1976 Sire 9299752, UK.

TANGERINE DREAM

835   <u>Phaedra</u>. 1974 Virgin VR-13108, US/ 1974 Virgin VI-2010, UK.

836   <u>Zeit</u>. 1972 Ohr OMM-256021, Germany/ 1976 Virgin VD-2503, UK.

Note: This group has a penchant for performing in cathedrals, appropriate to the Gothic overtones of their music.

TEN YEARS AFTER

837   "Classical thing." <u>Recorded live</u>. 1973 Columbia C2X-32288, US/ 1973 Chrysalis 1049, UK.

TRAFFIC

838   "No face, no name, and no number." <u>Mr. Fantasy</u>. 1968 United Artists UAS-6651, US/ 1967 Island ILPS-9061, UK.

Note: Baroque-type harpsichord can be heard in this song, which also appears on <u>Best of Traffic</u> (1970 United Artists UAS-5500, US/ 1969 Island ILPS-9112, UK) and <u>More heavy traffic</u> (1975 United Artists UA-LA526-G, US).

TRIUMVIRAT

(see also parts I and IIIA)

839   <u>Pompeii</u>. 1977 Capitol ST-11697 (SN-16120), US.

840   <u>Spartacus</u>. 1975 Capitol ST-11392, US/ 1975 Harvest SHSP-4048, UK.

U.K.

841   "Presto vivace and reprise." <u>U.K.</u>. 1978 Polydor PD-1-6146, US/ 1978 Polydor 2302-080, UK.

Note: Group members on this album came from King Crimson (John Wetton, Eddie Jobson), Yes (Bill Bruford), and Soft Machine (Allan Holdsworth).

ULTRAVOX

842   "Hymn." Quartet. 1983 Chrysalis B6V-41394, US/ 1982
       Chrysalis CHR-1394, UK.

       Note: The beginning of this song uses church-like
       harmonies and synthesized strings. The album was
       produced by George Martin.

843   "Vienna." Vienna. 1980 Chrysalis CHR-1296, US and
       UK.

       Note: This song features piano, viola, and violins.

UNITED STATES OF AMERICA

844   United States of America. 1968 Columbia CS-9619, US/
       1968 CBS 63340, UK.

       Note: Classically-trained musicians incorporate
       violins and Bartok-like styles with electronic music
       on this album.

VAN DER GRAAF GENERATOR

845   Pawn hearts. 1971 Charisma CH-1051, US/ 1972
       Charisma CAS-1051, UK.

VOLLENWEIDER, ANDREAS

846   Behind the gardens -- behind the wall -- under the
       tree ... . 1981 CBS FM-37793, US/ 1981 CBS 85545,
       UK.

       Note: Vollenweider performs on electracoustic
       modified pedal harp with woodwinds, guitars, and
       synthesizer.

847   Caverna magica (... under the tree -- in the cave
       ... . 1983 CBS FM-37827, US/ 1983 CBS 25980, UK.

WAKEMAN, RICK

       (see also parts I and IIIA)

848   The six wives of Henry VIII. 1973 A&M SP-4361, US/
       1973 A&M AMLH-64361, UK.

       Note: A single of "Anne/Catherine" was released
       (1973 A&M 1430, US).

WALLENSTEIN

849   Stories, songs & symphonies. 1975 (Ohr) Cosmic
       Courier/Metronome KM-58-014, Germany.

Note: This German band integrates guitar,
synthesizer, drums, violin, and percussion.

WAY, DARRYL

850   Concerto for electric violin and synthesizer.   1978
       Island ILPS-9550, UK.

Note: Darryl Way was a member of the rock group
Curved Air.

WEBBER, ANDREW LLOYD. See LLOYD-WEBBER, ANDREW

WHO

(see also part IIIA)

851   Tommy. 1969 Decca DXSW7-205, US/ 1969 Track 613-
       013/014, UK.

Contents: Overture -- It's a boy -- You didn't hear
it -- Amazing journey -- Sparks -- Eyesight to the
blind -- Christmas -- Cousin Kevin -- The acid queen
-- Underture -- Do you think it's alright -- Fiddle
about -- Pinball wizard -- There's a doctor I've
found -- Go to the mirror boy -- Tommy can you hear
me -- Smash the mirror -- Sensation -- Miracle cure
-- Sally Simpson -- I'm free -- Welcome -- Tommy's
holiday camp -- We're not gonna take it
Note: This "rock opera" incorporates the opera
elements of the overture, songs interspersed with
instrumental interludes, a story set to music, and
moral or character development. The album reached #4
on the Billboard pop album chart. The Who performed
Tommy live at the New York Metropolitan Opera House
June 7, 1970 and at various classical halls and opera
houses throughout Europe in 1969 and 1970. The
original Who-only version was reissued (1973 MCA
MCA2-10005, US/ 1971-72 Track 2406-007/008, UK). A
version by the London Symphony Orchestra with the Who
and guest soloists was performed (see 636). A
somewhat altered version of Tommy appeared as a
soundtrack album for the Ken Russell film (1975
Polydor PD2-9502, US/ 1975 Polydor 2657-014, UK).

WILLIAMS, MASON

852   "Baroque-a-nova." The Mason Williams phonograph
       record. 1968 Warner Bros. WS-1729, US (album);
       1968 Warner Bros. B-7235, US (single).

Note: The single reached #96 on the Billboard pop
singles chart.

853   "Classical gas." The Mason Williams phonograph
       record. 1968 Warner Bros. WS-1729, US (album);

1968 Warner Bros. B-7190, US/ 1968 Warner Bros.
WB-7190, UK (singles).

Note: The single reached #2 on the Billboard pop
singles chart and featured acoustic guitar, strings,
brass and percussion.

WONDER, STEVIE

(see also part I)

854 Journey through the secret life of plants. 1979
     Tamla T13-371C2, US/ 1979 Tamla TMSP-6009, UK.

855 "Village ghetto land." Songs in the key of life.
     1976 Tamla T13-340C2, US/ 1976 Tamla TMSP-6002, UK.

YAZ/YAZOO

856 "And on." You and me both. 1983 Sire 1-23903, US/
     1983 Mute STUMM-12, UK.

Note: Chime-like and harpsichord-like synthesizer
sounds are used on this song.

YES

(see also part I)

857 Close to the edge. 1972 Atlantic SD-7244 (SD-19133),
     US/ 1972 Atlantic K-50012, UK.

Note: This album reached #3 on the Billboard pop
album chart.

858 "Madrigal." Tormato. 1978 Atlantic SD-19202, US/
     1978 Atlantic K-50518, UK.

Note: Harpsichord played by Rick Wakeman is
prominent on this song.

859 Time and a word. 1970 Atlantic SD-8273, US/ 1970
     Atlantic 2400-006, UK.

Note: A small orchestra is incorporated into the
rock music on this album.

860 Tales from topographic oceans. 1973 Atlantic SD-2908,
     US/ 1973 Atlantic K-80001, UK.

Note: Mahlerian and Ives-like influences have been
described relating to this album, which reached #6 on
the Billboard pop album chart.

861 "Turn of the century." Going for the one. 1977
     Atlantic SD-19106, US/ 1977 Atlantic K-50379, UK.

ZAPPA, FRANK

(see also parts I and IIIA)

862 Orchestral favorites. 1979 DiscReet DSK-2294, US/
     1979 DiscReet K-59212, UK.

     Contents: Strictly genteel -- Pedro's dowry -- Naval
     aviation in art -- Duke of prunes -- Bogus pomp
     Note: Pieces on this album are composed by Frank
     Zappa and performed by a small rock orchestra.

     D. Rock Music Influences on Classical Music

1. Classical Composers

   BRANCA, GLENN

     863 The ascension. 1981 Nine Nine 99-001, US.

     864 Symphony no.3 (gloria). 1983 Neutral 4, US.
          Note: The two above albums were composed by an
          avant-garde classical composer using rock har-
          monics and overtones, hyperamplification, and
          exotically tuned guitars.

   GLASS, PHILIP

     865 Einstein on the beach. 1979 Tomato TOM-4-2901,
          US.

          Note: This is a rock-influenced minimalist opera
          by an avant-garde classical composer.

     866 Glassworks. 1982 CBS FM-37265, US/ 1982 CBS
          73640, UK.

     867 North Star. 1977 Virgin PZ-34669, US/ 1977
          Virgin VI-2085, UK.

          Note: Glass uses rock characteristics of
          repetition, heavy amplification and prominent
          rhythm.

     868 The photographer. 1983 CBS FM-37849, US/ 1983
          Epic EPC-25480, UK.

          Note: Rock-style videos were released from this
          mixed media theater piece for the song "A gentle-
          man's honor" and for "Photographer Act III."

   HENZE, HANS WERNER

     869 Musen Siziliens (Muses of Sicily). 1968 Deutsche
          Grammophon SLPM-139-374, Germany.

Note: Henze once suggested that his secular cantata was inspired by the rock group Rolling Stones.

2. Classical record packaging

FOX, VIRGIL

870 <u>Bach live at Fillmore East</u>. 1971 Decca DL-75263, US.

Note: Fox's albums featured psychedelic and rock-style album covers. His on-stage style and light-shows borrowed from rock concerts, even though the music was essentially straight.

871 <u>Heavy organ: Bach live at Winterland, San Francisco</u>. 1972 MCA DL-75323, US.

Note: Winterland and Fillmore East (above) were rock concert halls.

872 <u>Heavy organ at Carnegie Hall</u>. 1973 RCA Red Seal ARD1-0081, US.

873 <u>Into the classics</u>. 1974 Angel S-36065, US.

874 <u>The Virgil Fox Bach book</u>. 1974 RCA Red Seal ARL1-0476, US.

875 <u>Virgil Fox plays the classics--heavy to light</u>. 1972 Angel S-36052, US.

VARIOUS ORCHESTRAS

876 <u>Front populaire</u>. 1979 EMI SP-647, France.

Note: Various classical orchestras appear on this rock-style picture-disc, the first for a classical record.

877 <u>Go for baroque!: greatest hits of the 1700's!</u>. 1972 RCA VICS-1687, US.

878 <u>Greatest hits of 1720</u>. 1977 Columbia MX-34544, US.

Note: The cover is a hit chart à la <u>Billboard</u> magazine using music from 1720 instead of rock songs.

879 <u>Greatest hits of 1721</u>. 1980 Columbia M-35821, US.

880 <u>Greatest hits of 1790</u>. 1980 CBS Masterworks M-37216, US.

881   <u>Greatest hits of the 1850's</u>.   1972 RCA Red Seal
       LSC-3259, US.

       Note: This is a compilation of Liszt pieces.

882   Greatest hits series.   1969-71 Columbia, US.

       Note: The concept of "greatest hits" is essen-
       tially an idea borrowed from similar compilations
       of rock artists and groups.   Examples are:
       <u>Bach's greatest hits, vol. 1</u>.   1969 Columbia
       MS-7501.
       <u>Bach's greatest hits, vol. 2</u>.   1970 Columbia
       MS-7514.
       <u>Beethoven's greatest hits</u>.   1969 Columbia MS-
       7504.
       <u>Berlioz' greatest hits</u>.   1971 Columbia M-30384.
       <u>Bizet's greatest hits</u>.   1970 Columbia MS-7517.
       <u>Brahm's greatest hits</u>.   1971 Columbia M-30307.
       <u>Chopin's greatest hits</u>.   1969 Columbia MS-7506.
       <u>Dvorak's greatest hits</u>.   1970 Columbia MS-7524.
       <u>Gershwin's greatest hits</u>.   1970 Columbia MS-7518.
       <u>Grieg's greatest hits</u>.   1969 Columbia MS-7505.
       <u>Handel's greatest hits</u>.   1970 Columbia MS-7515.
       <u>Liszt's greatest hits</u>.   1971 Columbia M-30306.
       <u>Mendelssohn's greatest hits</u>.   1970 Columbia
       MS-7516.
       <u>Mozart's greatest hits</u>.   1969 Columbia MS-7507.
       <u>Prokofiev's greatest hits</u>.   1970 Columbia MS-
       7528.
       <u>Rachmaninoff's greatest hits</u>.   1969 Columbia
       MS-7508.
       <u>Ravel's greatest hits</u>.   1970 Columbia MS-7512.
       <u>Rimsky-Korsakov's greatest hits</u>.   1969 Columbia
       MS-7509.
       <u>Saint-Saens' greatest hits</u>.   1970 Columbia
       MS-7522.
       <u>Schubert's greatest hits</u>.   1970 Columbia MS-7526.
       <u>Sibelius' greatest hits</u>.   1970 Columbia MS-7527.
       <u>Johann Strauss' greatest hits</u>.   1969 Columbia
       MS-7502.
       <u>Tchaikovsky's greatest hits</u>.   1969 Columbia
       MS-7503.
       <u>Wagner's greatest hits</u>.   1969 Columbia MS-7511.

883   Greatest hits series.   1971-73 RCA Red Seal, US.

       Note: This series is similar to 882.   Examples
       are:
       <u>Bach's greatest hits, vol. 1</u>.   1971 RCA Red Seal
       LSC-5004.
       <u>Bach's greatest hits, vol. 2</u>.   1971 RCA Red Seal
       LSC-5015.
       <u>Beethoven's greatest hits</u>.   1971 RCA Red Seal
       LSC-5010.

Brahm's greatest hits. 1972 RCA Red Seal LSC-
  5021.
Chopin's greatest hits. 1972 RCA Red Seal
  LSC-5014.
Gershwin's greatest hits. 1971 RCA Red Seal
  LSC-5001.
Handel's greatest hits. 1973 RCA Red Seal
  ARL1-0110.
Liszt's greatest hits. 1973 RCA Red Seal ARL1-
  0111.
Mahler's greatest hits. 1971 RCA Red Seal
  LSC-5013.
Mendelssohn's greatest hits. 1972 RCA Red Seal
  LSC-5016.
Mozart's greatest hits. 1973 RCA Red Seal
  ARL1-0112.
Prokofiev's greatest hits. 1973 RCA Red Seal
  ARL1-0113.
Rachmaninoff's greatest hits. 1972 RCA Red Seal
  LSC-5000.
Ravel's greatest hits. 1971 RCA Red Seal LSC-
  5002.
Rimsky-Korsakov's greatest hits. 1971 RCA Red
  Seal LSC-5012.
Schubert's greatest hits. 1973 RCA Red Seal
  ARL1-0114.
Sibelius' greatest hits. 1973 RCA Red Seal
  ARL1-0115.
Johann Strauss' greatest hits. 1971 RCA Red Seal
  LSC-5005.
Richard Strauss' greatest hits. 1972 RCA Red
  Seal LSC-5019.
Stravinsky's greatest hits. 1972 RCA Red Seal
  LSC-5018.
Tchaikovsky's greatest hits. 1971 RCA Red Seal
  LSC-5008.
Verdi's greatest hits. 1972 RCA Red Seal LSC-
  5011.
Vivaldi's greatest hits. 1973 RCA Red Seal
  ARL1-0156.

884 Heavy hits: great music that inspired today's
     hits. 1971 RCA Red Seal LSC-3211, US.

     Contents: Strauss/Also sprach Zarathustra:
     opening fanfare -- Mozart/Piano concerto no. 21:
     andante -- Bach/Lute suite no. 1: bourrée --
     Satie/Gymnopédie no. 3 -- Bach/Brandenburg
     concerto no. 3: allegro -- Beethoven/Symphony
     no. 9: finale
     Note: These are straight classical versions.

885 Joy: great classics that inspired great pop and
     rock hits of the '60's and '70's. 1972 RCA Red
     Seal LSC-3290, US.

Contents: Bach/Jesu, joy of man's desiring --
Moussorgsky-Ravel/Pictures at an exhibition:
Baba Yaga's hut; Great gate at Kiev --
Tchaikovsky/The nutcracker: march -- Bach/Lute
suite no. 1: bourrée -- Satie/Gymnopédie no. 3
-- Bach/Minuet in G -- Brahms/Symphony no. 4:
allegro giocoso -- Mozart/Symphony no. 40: molto
allegro -- Beethoven/Symphony no. 9: ode to joy
Note: These are the original straight classical
versions.

886   Joy! The great composers' hits for the '70s.
      1972 Columbia M-31349, US.

Contents: Bach/Jesu, joy of man's desiring --
Bach/Minuet, from Little suite -- Purcell/Music
for the funeral of Queen Mary -- Rossini/The
thieving magpie overture -- Satie/Gymnopédie no.
3 -- Moussorgsky/The great gate of Kiev (from
Pictures at an exhibition) -- Rossini/William
Tell overture -- Mozart/Theme from Elvira
Madigan (Andante from piano concerto no. 21) --
Mozart/First movement from symphony no. 40 --
Beethoven/Choral finale from symphony no. 9
Note: These are the original straight classical
versions.

887   Orphic Egg composer series. 1972-73 Orphic
      Egg/London, US.

Note: The albums in this series contain straight
classical performances by various orchestras.
The album jackets feature psychedelic cover art
and some have hip street talk liner notes by rock
critics. The series includes:
Bach's head. 1972 Orphic Egg OES-6902
Beethoven's head. 1972 Orphic Egg OES-6904
Mahler's head. 1972 Orphic Egg OES-6901
Moussorgsky's head. 1973 Orphic Egg OES-6910
Mozart's head. 1972 Orphic Egg OES-6903
The musical head. 1972 Orphic Egg OES-6900
Prokofiev's head. 1972 Orphic Egg OES-6906
Ravel's head. 1972 Orphic Egg OES-6905
Stravinsky's head. 1972 Orphic Egg OES-6907

888   Solid gold baroque. 1982 Vanguard SRV-376SD, US.

Note: This album includes straight popular
baroque pieces by Bach, Handel, Vivaldi, etc.
packaged like rock "gold" hits.

889   Switched-off Bach. 1969 Columbia MS-7241, US.

Note: This album features straight orchestra
versions of the same pieces which appear on
Walter Carlos' synthesizer album Switched-on Bach
(see part I).

3. Rock Artists Appearing in Straight Classical Roles

BOWIE, DAVID

890 The civil wars. 1984 ?, US.

Note: A recording was supposedly made of this
Robert Wilson opera in September of 1983, but it
has not been released yet. The work's première
was to have been June 6-9, 1984 at the Olympic
Arts Festival in Los Angeles, but it was can-
celled due to lack of funds. David Bowie was
reported to have the part of Abraham Lincoln in
this twelve hour opera. Collaborators in the
project were Philip Glass and David Byrne (of
rock group Talking Heads).

891 Peter and the wolf. 1978 RCA Red Seal ARL1-2743,
US.

Note: David Bowie narrates while the Philadelphia Orchestra handles the music of Prokofiev.

BYRNE, DAVID

892 The Catherine Wheel. 1981 Sire M5S-3645, US
(cassette).

Note: Byrne, of the rock group Talking Heads,
composed and performed the music for this modern
ballet by the Twyla Tharp troupe. The entire
score is available on cassette only. Excerpts
appear on Songs from the Broadway production of
"The Catherine Wheel" (1981 Sire SRK-3645, US).
Although the music is more rock than classical,
the unusual idea of a rock musician being commis-
sioned to score a ballet is more classical in
nature.

The civil wars. See 890

DALTREY, ROGER

893 The beggar's opera. 1983 BBC, UK.

Note: Daltrey, well-known singer of the rock
group Who, sang the part of Macheath in a BBC
broadcast of the 1728 ballad opera by Pepusch/
Gay.

LEER, THIJS VAN

894 Introspection. 1973 Columbia KC-32346, US/ 1972
CBS 65589, UK.

Note: Classically trained van Leer, a member of rock group Focus, performs some straight classical versions of Fauré and Bach on flute with an orchestra.

895   Introspection 2.   1976 Columbia M-34510, US/ 1975 CBS 65913, UK.

Note: Flute and orchestra again team for some straight classical pieces by Granados, Cimarosa, Bach, and Handel.

RONSTADT, LINDA

896   The pirates of Penzance.   1981 Elektra VE-601, US.

Note: Ronstadt starred in this recording of the 1981 Broadway production of Gilbert and Sullivan's operetta. A film was also released.

897   La Bohème.

Note: Ronstadt stars as Mimi in a November-December 1984 production of this of Puccini opera at the New York Public Theater. A synthesizer replaces much of the string section of the orchestra and the English libretto has been somewhat modernized, while maintaining the integrity of the piece.

STREISAND, BARBRA

898   Classical Barbra.   1976 Columbia M-33452, US.

Note: Streisand has at times been considered a rock singer, especially in the 1970's, but on this album she performs straight classical versions of songs by Debussy, Canteloube, Wolf, Fauré, Orff, Handel, Schumann, and Ogerman.

Appendix A.
Selected Big Band
Versions of the Classics

Dorsey, Tommy. The complete Tommy Dorsey, vol. 4 (1937).
1979 Bluebird/RCA AXM2-5564, US.

    Relevant contents: Humoresque (Dvorak) -- Barcarolle
(Offenbach) -- Hymn to the sun (Rimsky-Korsakov) --
Rollin' home (Dvorak)

Ellington, Duke. Duke Ellington and his orchestra. 1968
Columbia Jazz Odyssey 3216-0252, US.

    Note: This album features transcriptions of sections of
Tchaikovsky's Nutcracker suite and Grieg's Peer Gynt
Suites no. 1 and 2.

Kenton, Stan. Kenton plays Wagner. 1965 Capitol STAO-2217,
US.

    Note: This album includes versions of Wagner's Tristan
und Isolde, Ride of the Valkyries, and Lohengrin.

Kirby, John. The biggest little band: 1937-41. 1978
Smithsonian Collection R-013, US.

    Relevant contents: Opus 5 (Chopin) -- Serenade (Schubert)
-- Beethoven riffs on (Beethoven)

Martin, Freddy. The best of Freddy Martin. 1975 MCA
MCA2-4080, US.

Martin, Freddy. Freddy Martin's greatest hits. 19?? Decca
DL-74908, US.

    Relevant contents (on both of above albums): Tonight we
love (Tchaikovsky) -- Bumble boogie (Rimsky-Korsakov) --
Piano concerto in A minor (Grieg)

Rogers, Shorty. <u>Swingin' nutcracker</u>.   1960 RCA LPM-2110
(mono), LSP-2110 (stereo), US.

Note: This is a version of Tchaikovsky's <u>Nutcracker
suite</u>.

<u>Swingin' the classics</u>.   1981 CBS P3-16175-CSP, US.

Partial contents: Bizet has his day (Bizet/Les Brown) --
Humoresque (Dvorak/Glenn Miller) -- Sabre dance
(Khatchaturian/Woody Herman) -- Spring song (Mendelssohn/
Benny Goodman) -- Flight of the bumblebee (Rimsky-
Korsakov/Harry James)

Appendix B.
Selected Jazz Versions
of the Classics

Bénichou, André. <u>Jazz guitar Bach</u>. 1965 Nonesuch H-1069 (mono), H-71069 (stereo), US.

Brubeck, Dave. "Blue rondo à la turk." <u>Time out</u>. 1960 Columbia CS-8192, US.

   Note: This piece uses rondo form and Turkish folk rhythms, but not the actual Mozart theme.

Classicats. <u>Bridging the gap</u>. 1970 Orion ORS-7033, US.

   Note: Selections from Bach's <u>Well-tempered clavier</u> are performed first in the original version on harpsichord, then in a jazz version.

Cole, Nat King. "Prelude in C sharp minor." <u>Trio days</u>. 1972 Capitol M-11033, US. (Rachmaninoff)

Gruntz, George. <u>Bach humbug!</u> 1964 Philips PHM-200-162 (mono), PHS-600-162 (stereo), US.

James, Bob. "Night on bald mountain." <u>One</u>. 1974 Columbia FC-36835, US (album); 1974 CTI 23, US (single). (Moussorgsky)

Laws, Hubert. <u>Afro-classic</u>. 1970 CTI CTI-6006, US.

   Relevant contents: Allegro from concerto #3 in D (J. S. Bach) -- Passacaglia in C minor (J. S. Bach) -- Flute sonata in F (Mozart)

Laws, Hubert. The rite of spring. 1971 CTI CTI-6012, US.

   Contents: Rite of spring (Stravinsky) -- Pavane (Fauré)
   -- Syrinx (Debussy) -- Brandenburg concerto no. 3, mvt. 1
   & 2 (J. S. Bach)

Laws, Hubert. The San Francisco concert. 1977 CTI CTI-
   7071, US.

   Relevant contents: Farandole, from L'Arlesienne suite no.
   2 (Bizet) -- Scheherazade (Rimsky-Korsakov)
   Note: Hubert Laws is joined by Bob James and others,
   supplemented by members of the San Francisco Symphony
   Orchestra.

Loffler, Franz. 300 year old goodies all jazzed up. 1965
   Mercury MG-21044, US.

   Partial contents: Bach's mashed bourrée -- Swingin' Bach
   -- Sorry Mr. Brubeck, it's Bach

Loussier, Jacques. Play Bach [no. 1-6]. 1959-64 London
   PS-287, 288, 289, 365, 454, 524, US.

Mann, Herbie. "Gymnopédie, by Erik Satie." Nirvana. 1965
   Atlantic SD-1426, US.

Modern Jazz Quartet. Collaboration. 1966 Atlantic SD-1429,
   US.

   Relevant contents: Fugue in A minor (J. S. Bach) --
   Concerto de Aranjuez (Rodrigo)

New Swingle Singers. Folio. 1980 Moss Music Group
   MMG-1125, US.

Schifrin, Lalo. The dissection and reconstruction of music
   from the past. 1966 Verve V6-8654, US.

Smith, Jimmy. Peter and the wolf. 1967 Verve V6-8652,
   SVLP-9159, US. (Prokofiev)

Swingle Singers. Anyone for Mozart?. 1965 Philips PHS-
   600-149, US.

Swingle Singers. Back to Bach. 1969 Philips PHS-600-288,
   US.

Swingle Singers. Bach's greatest hits. 1963 Philips
  PHS-600-097, US.

Swingle Singers. Getting romantic. 1965 Philips PHS-600-
  191, US.

Swingle Singers. Going baroque. 1965 Philips PHM-200-126
  (mono), PHS-600-126 (stereo), US.

Swingle Singers. Rococo à go go. 1965 Philips PHM-200-214
  (mono), PHS-600-214 (stereo), US.

Swingle Singers. Spanish masters. 1968 Philips PHS-600-
  261, US.

Swingle Singers. Swingin' Mozart no. 3. 1965 Philips
  110072, US.

Swingle II. Love songs for madrigals and madriguys. 1974
  Columbia M-33013 (PC-34194), US.

Swingle II. Swingle II. 1977 RCA Red Seal RL-25112, US.

Wayland Quartet. Jazz loves Bach. 1966 Four Corners of the
  World FCS-4249, US.

Winter, Paul, Consort. Something in the wind. 196? A&M
  SP-4207, US.

  Relevant contents: Cantata 127 (J. S. Bach) -- Le tombeau
  de Couperin (Ravel) -- The Indians (Ives) -- Ayre on a
  g-string (J. S. Bach)

Appendix C.
Selected Parodies
of the Classics

Jones, Spike. <u>Dinner music for people who aren't very</u>
<u>hungry</u>. 19?? Verve MGV-4005, US.

    Partial contents: Brahm's alibi -- Pal-yat-chee

Jones, Spike. <u>Spike Jones is murdering the classics</u>. 1971
RCA Red Seal LSC-3235(e), AGL1-4142(e), US.

    Contents: Pal-yat-chee -- Liebestraum -- The blue Danube
    -- The Jones laughing record -- Nutcracker suite -- Dance
    of the hours -- None but the lonely heart -- Morpheus --
    Ill barkio -- Carmen

Portsmouth Sinfonia. <u>The Portsmouth Sinfonia plays the</u>
<u>popular classics</u>. 1973 Columbia KC-33049, US.

Russell, Anna. <u>The Anna Russell album?</u>. 1972 Columbia
MG-31199, US.

Russell, Anna. <u>Anna Russell sings?</u>. 1952 Columbia ML-4594,
US.

Russell, Anna. <u>Anna Russell sings! Again?</u>. 1953 Columbia
ML-4733, US.

Schickele, Peter. <u>P.D.Q. Bach: an hysteric return</u>. 1966
Vanguard VSD-79223, US.

    Partial contents: Unbegun symphony -- The seasonings --
    Okay chorale

Schickele, Peter. <u>P.D.Q. Bach: music you can't get out of</u>
<u>your head</u>. 1982 Vanguard VSD-79443, US.

Partial contents: Howdy symphony -- Suite from "The civilian barber"

Schickele, Peter. <u>Peter Schickele presenting P.D.Q. Bach (1807-1742?)</u>. 1965 Vanguard VSD-79195, US.

Partial contents: Concerto for horn and hardart -- Iphigenia in Brooklyn

Schickele, Peter. <u>The wurst of P.D.Q. Bach</u>. 1971 Vanguard VSD-719/720, US.

Sherman, Allan. "Hello muddah, hello faddah." 1963 Warner Bros. 5378, US/ 1963 Warner Bros. WB-106, UK (singles).

Note: This song is based on Ponchielli's "Dance of the hours" and also appears on <u>The best of Allan Sherman</u> (1979 Rhino RNLP-005, US).

Valjean. <u>Mashin' the "classicks"</u>. 196? Carlton STLP-146, US.

Contents: Mr. Mozart's mash (Mozart) -- Bird mash (Mendelssohn) -- Mashanova (Rubenstein) -- Little mash muffet (Haydn) -- Hungarian mash #5 (Brahms) -- The minute mash (Chopin) -- Mashville, U.S.A. (Liszt) -- Mash militaire (Schubert) -- Two for the mash (Mendelssohn) -- Mashacre in G (Beethoven) -- Mashmellow pudding (Mozart) -- Mashing along (Tchaikovsky)

Appendix D.
Selected Country and Folk Versions of the Classics

Anger, Darol. "Bach partita #3 in E major." <u>The duo</u>. 1983 Rounder 0168, US.

    Note: This bluegrass version is performed on mandolin.

Crary, Dan. "Memories of Mozart." <u>Guitar</u>. 1983 Sugar Hill SH-3730, US.

    Note: Bluegrass-style guitar is featured on this recording.

De Danann. "The arrival of the Queen of Sheba (in Galway)." <u>Song for Ireland</u>. 1983 Sugar Hill SH-1130, US.

    Note: This Irish traditional band performs a version of Handel.

First Nashville Guitar Quartet. "Brandenburg." <u>The First Nashville Guitar Quartet</u>. 1979 RCA AHL1-3302, AYL1-3741, US. (Bach)

Garrett, Snuff. <u>Classical country</u>. 1976 Ranwood R-8156, US.

Jernigan, Doug. "Jesu, joy of man's desiring." <u>Roadside rag</u>. 1976 Flying Fish 024, US.

    Note: This is a steel guitar version of Bach.

Kottke, Leo. "Bourrée." <u>Mudlark</u>. 1971 Capitol ST-682, US.

    Note: This acoustic guitar version of Bach also appears on <u>The best</u> (1978 Capitol SWBC-11867, US).

Kottke, Leo. "Jesu, joy of man's desiring." My feet are smiling. 1973 Capitol ST-11164, US.

   Note: This acoustic guitar version of Bach also appears on The best (1978 Capitol SWBC-11867, US).

Kottke, Leo. "The Scarlatti rip-off." Chewing pine. 1975 Capitol ST-11446, US.

   Note: This acoustic guitar piece also appears on 1971-1976 (1976 Capitol ST-11576, US).

Muldaur, Geoff. Geoff Muldaur and Amos Garrett. 1978 Flying Fish 061, US.

   Relevant contents: Dance of the sugar plum fairy (Tchaikovsky) -- Prelude in Em, no. 4, opus 28 (Chopin)

Nitty Gritty Dirt Band. "Gavotte no. 2." Dirt, silver and gold. 1977 United Artists 9802 (LA-670), US.

   Note: This Bach piece is performed on acoustic guitar.

Reid, Harvey. "Minuet in G." Nothin' but guitar. 1982 Woodpecker 101, US.

   Note: Solo acoustic guitar is featured on this piece.

Steeleye Span. "Bach goes to Limerick." Commoner's crown. 1975 Chrysalis CHR-1071, US and UK.

   Note: An Irish folk style is used in this piece.

Index

Note: Numbers in this index refer to entry numbers. The general index covers rock artists, rock groups, orchestras, choruses, classical composers, producers, conductors, and song or instrumental titles. Album titles are not indexed. Some songs and instrumentals may have titles indexed by commonly known classical nicknames (e.g., "Flight of the bumblebee") if that is the title used on the recording, but not all such pieces based on the same theme have the same title. There-fore, the classical composer's name should be consulted in the index in order to locate all versions of the piece. Under the composer's name, some works have been sectioned out when they have been borrowed more often than the others, but generally the works are gathered together in one entry number sequence. Alphabetization is generally word by word. Mac and Mc are listed as spelled, not mixed. Number sequences after a common initial word or words are in numerical order. Abbrevia-tions (e.g. Mr., no.) are listed as spelled. Acronyms are listed at the beginning of their respective alphabetical sections.

"Atom heart mother suite,"
619
Auger, Brian, and the
Trinity, 022-023
"Auntie Gin's theme," 539
"Autumn," 826
"Ave Maria" (Bach/Gounod),
122
"Ave Maria" (Schubert), 123,
458
"Ave rock Maria," 325
Axelrod, David, 024, 728

BS&T String Ensemble, 701
B. Bumble and the Stingers.
See Bumble, B., and the
Stingers
"B minor mass," 045
"Baby, I love you," 524
"Baby, let's smooth it
over," 554
"Baby love," 554
"Baby you're a rich man,"
498
Bach, Johann Sebastian, 034,
039, 045-048, 053-056,
066-072, 076, 081-084,
086, 090-091, 110, 116,
122, 125, 133, 136, 138,
141-142, 148, 151, 154,
170, 179, 224, 242, 254,
272, 276, 278, 280-282,
286-288, 294-298, 300,
309, 324-325, 334, 347,
353, 356, 367, 373, 375,
411, 419, 428, 440,
459-460, 490, 604-605,
803, 870-871, 874,
882-889, 894-895;
    Air for the G string:
    004, 065, 121, 254,
    297, 318, 324, 367;
    Jesu, joy of man's
    desiring: 008, 062,
    075, 106, 432, 469D,
    885-886;
    Toccata and fugue in D
    minor: 153, 243, 261,
    267, 271, 330, 364
"Bach a 'Sinding," 110
"Bach onto this," 242
"Bach two part invention in
D minor," 170
"Bachmania," 106
"Bach's prelude," 428

"Back in my arms again," 554
"Back seat of my car," 582
Back-Beat Philharmonic, 688
"Baker Street," 527, 529
"Ballad of John and Yoko,
The," 482
"Ballet for a girl in
Buchannon," 706
"Ballet-volta," 355
Baltimore Symphony, 658
"Bamba, La," 551
"Bangladesh," 499
"Barbarian, The," 171, 181
"Barber of Seville," 207
"Barbero, El," 124
Barclay James Harvest, 641,
689-690
Barclay James Harvest
Symphony Orchestra, 641
"Baroque connection, The,"
276
Baroque Ensemble of the
Merseyside Kammermusik-
Gesellschaft, 571
Baroque Inevitable, 472
Baroque Pops, 025-026
"Baroque-a-nova," 852
Baroques, 691
Bartok, Bela, 057, 171, 490,
844
Bass, Sid, 027-028
Batt, Mike, 586-588
"Battle, The," 631
Bavarian String Ensemble,
623
Baxter, Bruce, 473
Baxter, Les, 029-037
"Be true to your school,"
494
Beach Boys, 038, 493-494,
509, 521, 531, 557, 566,
692-693
Beatles, 039-042, 470, 472,
474, 480-482, 486,
488-490, 492, 495-499,
503, 505-510, 515,
522-523, 527-529, 531,
535-543, 549, 551, 558,
562, 564, 568, 571, 574,
578, 581, 584, 584A, 585,
589, 694-698. See also
Harrison, George; Lennon,
John; McCartney, Paul;
Starr, Ringo
"Beatles concerto, The," 574
Beatles Cracker Suite, 474

About the Author

JANELL R. DUXBURY is a Library Associate 2 for Acquisitions in the Memorial Library of the University of Wisconsin, Madison.